C000292053

The Handbook for DofE Leaders

This *Handbook* provides advice and guidance for Duke of Edinburgh's Award (DofE) Leaders to set up and run a DofE group.

The Duke of Edinburgh's Award is a voluntary, non-competitive programme of activities for anyone aged 14-24. Doing their DofE gives young people the opportunity to experience new activities or develop existing skills. There are three progressive levels of programmes which when successfully completed lead to a Bronze, Silver or Gold Award. Young people create their own DofE programme by choosing a volunteering, physical and skills activity, going on an expedition and, for their Gold only, taking part in a residential activity.

The Duke of Edinburgh's Award is a national youth charity that operates throughout the UK. Founded by HRH The Duke of Edinburgh in 1956, DofE programmes are now delivered under licence by almost 500 partners who offer it through DofE groups in youth clubs, voluntary organisations, schools, colleges, young offender institutions, housing associations and businesses.

Currently over 275,000 young people are doing their DofE in the UK, and over 80,000 achieve a Bronze, Silver or Gold Award each year. They are supported by over 45,000 Leaders.

Our mission
To inspire, guide and support young people in their self-development and recognise their achievements.

Foreword

Young people growing up in this modern, complicated world have many difficulties to face, and opportunities for personal achievement are often limited. At the same time, parents, teachers, voluntary organisation leaders and employers, who recognise their responsibilities towards young people, also have their challenges.

This programme is intended to help both the young as well as those who are concerned for their welfare. The object is to provide an introduction to worthwhile leisure activities and voluntary service; as a challenge to the individual to discover the satisfaction of achievement and as a guide for those people and organisations who would like to encourage the development of their younger fellow citizens.

I hope that all those who take part in this programme will find an added purpose and pleasure in their lives. I am quite sure that all those who help to run it will gain that special sense of satisfaction which comes from helping others to discover hidden abilities and to overcome a challenge.

Introduction
from Debra Searle MBE, Trustee

The Duke of Edinburgh's Award (DofE) enables a young person to develop their mind, body and soul in a non-competitive environment. Its ability to elevate their self-confidence, skills and aspirations should never be underestimated, as I discovered for myself while undertaking my Gold programme. The whole experience had an amazing influence on my life and I enjoyed every section.

The Expedition section was life-changing for me and ignited a passion in me to become a professional adventurer. It is a career I have enjoyed for many years now. Without the chance to prove myself through achieving my Gold Award I doubt I would have rowed the Atlantic single-handed, sailed around Antarctica or completed the world's longest canoe race. I still use the skills today that my DofE Leader taught me all those years ago on Dartmoor.

The Volunteering section of my Gold also taught me valuable lessons about the importance of giving back to the community and this has stayed with me into adulthood. I was delighted to learn recently that I am not alone and that a wonderful 61% of Award holders go on to volunteer in their local community. It's also incredible to think that our young people give an equivalent value of £21 million a year to local communities through their volunteering activities.

Just imagine what an impact it would have on our society and the economy if every young person in the UK had the opportunity to have a DofE volunteering experience. It is aspirations like this that inspire me to commit wholeheartedly to volunteering as a DofE Trustee for the Charity.

I am just one of millions of people who have been privileged to have experienced DofE programmes, thanks to the generosity of volunteers and supporting organisations. None of this would be possible without you. I would like to thank and congratulate you if you are a DofE Leader or if you are considering becoming one and joining us in our work. Your much appreciated commitment is helping to ensure a positive and meaningful difference to the lives of hundreds of thousands of young people.

This *Handbook* should tell you everything you need to know about The Duke of Edinburgh's Award; its structure, the programmes, how to run and maintain a group and your role as a Leader.

Please do make the most of your time with us. Like the young people you will lead, you too are about to embark on an adventure that will fill you with unique experiences, memories and a genuine sense of achievement. Thank you and best wishes in your endeavours.

Debra Searle

Contents

Chapter 1: Introducing The Duke of Edinburgh's Award

Chapter 2: Starting and leading a DofE group

Chapter 3: DofE programmes

Chapter 4: The sections in detail

Chapter 5: Completion, recognition and progression

Chapter 6: Other important information and sources of support

Appendices

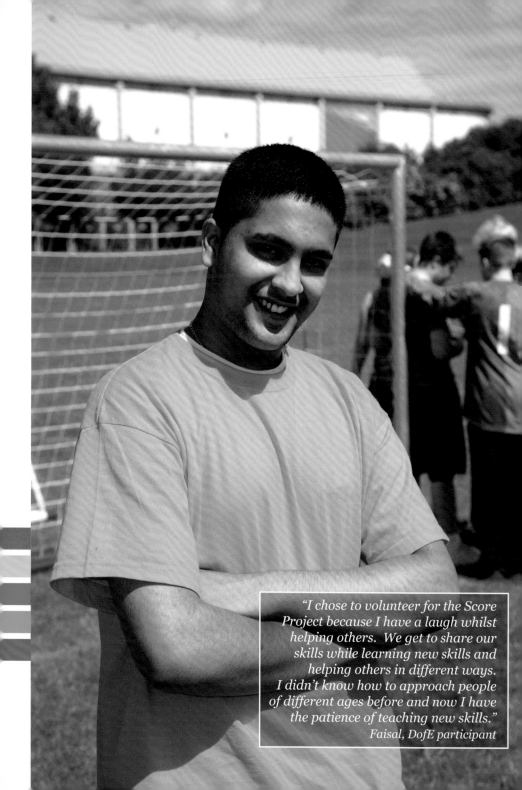

"I chose to volunteer for the Score Project because I have a laugh whilst helping others. We get to share our skills while learning new skills and helping others in different ways. I didn't know how to approach people of different ages before and now I have the patience of teaching new skills."

Faisal, DofE participant

Chapter 1
Introducing The Duke of Edinburgh's Award

Whilst having a passion for helping young people to achieve is essential, so too is understanding the way in which we help people and work with others.

This *Handbook* will provide you with all the information you need to be a DofE Leader and run DofE programmes with your group. Read on and you'll discover how the DofE works, what your responsibilities are as a Leader and how we can support you in your work.

Please do take the time to familiarise yourself with its contents as it is essential that everyone involved in the delivery of DofE programmes offer consistently high levels of service and support. This ensures that all participants receive a high quality, enjoyable and safe DofE experience that is personal to them.

Thank you for offering your time to be a Leader; it means so much to both our participants and The Duke of Edinburgh's Award Charity. Your commitment and efforts are greatly appreciated.

D*of*E programmes

The concept of the DofE is simple – anyone aged between 14 and 24 can do a programme at one of three progressive levels which, when successfully completed, lead to a Bronze, Silver or Gold Duke of Edinburgh's Award.

There are four sections at Bronze and Silver level and five at Gold. With your assistance, participants select and set their own overall timescales and programme objectives in each of the following areas:

Volunteering: undertaking service to individuals or the community.

Physical: improving in an area of sport, dance or fitness activities.

Skills: developing practical and social skills and personal interests.

Expedition: planning, training for and completion of an adventurous journey in the UK or abroad.

At Gold level, participants must do an additional fifth **Residential** section, which involves staying and working away from home doing a shared activity.

Each section must be done for a minimum period of time. It must be monitored and then assessed by someone with knowledge of that particular activity to achieve an Award.

Each progressive level demands more time and commitment from participants.

Our guiding principles

At the DofE we strive to achieve our mission through personal development programmes and the assessment and presentation of Awards.

All our programmes are driven by the following ten guiding principles, which are at the heart of everything we do.

1: Non-competitive

A DofE programme is a personal challenge and not a competition against others. Every participant's programme is tailor-made to reflect their individual starting point, abilities and interests.

2: Achievable by all

A Duke of Edinburgh's Award is achievable by any young person who chooses to take up its challenge, regardless of ability, gender, background or location.

3: Voluntary

Whilst DofE programmes may be offered within school, college, work time, custody or extra-curricular activity, young people choose to do a programme and commit some of their free time to undertake their activities.

4: Personal development

A DofE programme inspires personal and social development. The value to young people is dependent on personal commitment, the learning process and the quality of the experience.

5: Personalised

Young people design their own programme, which can be tailored to suit their personal circumstances, choices and local provision. They start at whichever level suits them best and they can take as long as they wish (within the age limits) to achieve an Award.

6: Balanced

Our aim is to ensure that participants experience development of the whole person; mind, body and soul. By undertaking activities focusing on at least four different aspects of development, young people complete a balanced and wide-ranging programme.

7: Progressive

At each level of engagement, a DofE programme demands progressively more time, commitment and responsibility from the participant.

8: Achievement focused

Before starting an activity, young people are encouraged to set their own challenging goals. If they aim for these goals and show improvement they will achieve a Duke of Edinburgh's Award.

9: Demand commitment

A DofE programme demands persistence and commitment and cannot be completed with a short burst of enthusiasm. Participants are encouraged to continue with activities and to maintain their interest beyond their programme requirements.

10: Enjoyable

Young people and Leaders should find participation enjoyable, fulfilling and rewarding.

The benefits

There are so many rewards for young people who do DofE programmes and achieve an Award. Its balanced programme of activities develops the whole person – mind, body and soul, in an environment of social interaction and team working.

Furthermore, as doing their DofE involves developing a personal programme of challenging activities, participants will enjoy unique experiences and rewards. In addition, the skills and personal attributes developed through participation are recognised by employers, colleges and universities. Having spoken with Award holders there is general agreement that participation develops:

- Self-belief
- Self-confidence
- A sense of identity
- Independence of thought and action
- Respect and understanding of people from different backgrounds, cultures and walks of life

- A sense of responsibility
- An awareness of their potential
- New talents and abilities
- An understanding of strengths and weaknesses
- The ability to plan and use time effectively
- The ability to learn from and give to others in the community
- New relationships
- Skills including problem solving, presentation and communication
- The ability to lead and work as part of a team.

There are plenty of benefits for you too. You'll have the satisfaction of knowing you have made a difference to someone's life. You'll see that glow and sense of pride participants have when they realise they've just done something they never imagined they could do.

And, of course, you'll play a pivotal role in helping a young person to develop the skills and attitudes they need to succeed in life. Ask any DofE Leader and they'll tell you that gives them an unbeatable sense of achievement.

Our structure

A wide range of organisations run DofE programmes. After satisfying a number of conditions, they are granted a licence to do so. Accordingly, the collective term for them is Licensed Organisation (LO). The diagram below illustrates the different types of Licensed Organisation:

Definitions

OA: An Operating Authority (OA) is a type of Licensed Organisation which holds the licence to deliver DofE programmes in a specified geographic area (though there may be other Licensed Organisations within this area). Operating Authority licences are often held by local authorities which offer DofE programmes through their youth services and which support a range of DofE centres in their area.

NOA: A National Operating Authority (NOA) is a type of Licensed Organisation which holds a licence to deliver DofE programmes to the young people with whom they work in one or more of the UK nations. Examples include Mencap, The Scout Association and the Air Training Corps.

DLC: A Directly Licensed Centre (DLC) is a type of Licensed Organisation which holds a licence to deliver DofE programmes to young people on its own premises. Directly Licensed Centres can include, for example, schools, academies, colleges, youth clubs and young offender institutions, which do not run their DofE provision under a licence provided by an Operating Authority.

DofE Business Partner: A DofE Business Partner is a type of Licensed Organisation which offers a DofE programme to a number of its employees.

All of the different types of Licensed Organisation are structured in a similar way.

The chart below outlines how the DofE is structured. Please familiarise yourself with this as we will refer to these roles throughout this *Handbook*.

Organisation:

Person:

DofE group
A group of ideally 15-20 young people who are working on their DofE programmes together with one DofE Leader. In a large DofE centre they may be grouped by peer groups, ages or levels (i.e. Bronze, Silver, Gold). Groups may be split into teams for certain activities, i.e. volunteering or their expedition.

DofE Leader
The adult responsible for a DofE group. They lead, guide and encourage young people, agree their programme choices and sign off evidence and sections in eDofE (our online programme management system). They may have other adults (helpers) who assist them.

DofE centre
The location where the DofE is run, for example, a school, youth centre, young offender institution. There may be one or more groups at a centre depending on the size of the centre/number of participants. This may be different for a uniformed group like the Scouts or Cadets.

DofE Co-ordinator
This person sets up and manages the DofE in a centre. They support Leaders and oversee the groups.

Licensed Organisation (LO)
The Licensed Organisation holds the licence to manage the delivery of DofE programmes and verify Awards.

DofE Manager
The person in an LO who is responsible for the day-to-day delivery of the DofE. A DofE centre's contact may be a local Co-ordinator or administrator within the Licensed Organisation rather than the DofE Manager. There will often be other assistants and staff involved.

The DofE Charity
Head Office and Regional/Country Offices deal with overall policy and central administration. A Board of Trustees governs the DofE Charity. It determines the criteria and maintains the integrity and quality of The Duke of Edinburgh's Award.

Trustees and approximately 100 staff
A Licensed Organisation will mainly have contact with the DofE Regional/Country Office or, in the case of National Operating Authorities, with Head Office.

Please note, these roles are not mutually exclusive. For example:
- *In a small centre there may only be one group and therefore, as a Leader, you may also assume the Co-ordinator role.*
- *A school that holds its own licence will be both the LO and the DofE centre. In this case, the DofE Manager and Co-ordinator is likely to be the same person, with other DofE Leaders involved with groups.*

The Handbook for *DofE* Leaders

In the UK there are almost 500 Licensed Organisations.

DofE programmes are run in over 10,500 DofE centres including: voluntary and community organisations, academies, secondary, independent and special schools, colleges and universities, young offender institutions, pupil referral units, housing associations, open DofE groups and businesses.

Your Licensed Organisation (LO)

Every centre and group must be authorised by a Licensed Organisation (LO) and the DofE Manager will be your main contact and source of support.
To get a licence, LOs must satisfy us that they understand the full implications of running DofE programmes.

They must:
- Be able to safeguard young people

- Maintain the DofE's aims and standards
- Have relevant policies and procedures in place
- Have an administrative framework to function correctly and ensure continuity.

As part of their licence renewal process, Licensed Organisations monitor quality levels in the delivery of the DofE within their authorised centres/groups.

Evidencing a high quality experience for young people is necessary to support this process. Further information on possible methods of monitoring and evaluating performance can be obtained from your DofE Manager.

Please see chapter six for full details of your Licensed Organisation's responsibilities and the support it can give you.

"It's great to see the students get enthusiastic. One of the most rewarding things is watching them struggling and overcoming it. It's good to see them put in situations that they'd never have otherwise been involved in like the expedition and volunteering – it makes them realise how lucky they are."
Julie Balchin, DofE Leader

Chapter 2
Starting and leading a DofE group

From the skills you need to be a Leader through to your ongoing responsibilities, this chapter takes you through the basics of starting and leading a DofE group.

What makes a DofE Leader?

Almost anyone with the desire to help young people develop can be a DofE Leader. We don't expect you to be able to climb mountains or survive for days in the wild. In fact you don't need any special skills or qualifications at all. If you do have a particular talent, we see that as a bonus.

The most important thing we look for is whether you really get a buzz out of helping young people improve themselves. Because, if you have that, your Licensed Organisation (LO) will provide the training and support you need.

Licensed Organisations and the DofE have safeguarding and child protection policies and procedures that include vetting the suitability of Co-ordinators, Leaders and any other adult helpers as part of the recruitment process. Your LO or DofE Co-ordinator will explain this and help you complete the relevant checks before you become involved.

> *"I love working with young people and the fact that it gives them so much. It is a wonderful programme for them and I think so much of it."*
> Sue Rose, DofE Leader

Your role and responsibilities

As a DofE Leader you play a crucial role in the success of your DofE group and participants' programmes. You are its focus and manager. Success will be made easier with the support of other adult helpers. You and/or your DofE Co-ordinator will need to recruit and train them, encourage teamwork and delegate responsibility.

You'll find a list of key DofE Leader responsibilities below. Whilst you can choose to delegate them amongst your team of helpers, it's important that they are all done.

Safeguarding participants is paramount

The safety and welfare of your group's participants is your primary concern at all times. Licensed Organisations and The Duke of Edinburgh's Award have safeguarding and child protection policies and procedures that you must adhere to.

For further information on the Code of Behaviour for DofE Leaders and helpers see chapter six, page 118.

Given the scope and breadth of DofE programmes, participants may undertake activities that are not directly managed or organised by your group, centre or LO. In such cases, parents and guardians of those under 18 must be informed that it is their responsibility (not yours) to ensure the activity is appropriately managed and insured.

Make it enjoyable and successful

Your role is to encourage and inspire young people at every stage of their adventure. From getting their interest in the first place and helping them choose activities which interest them to helping them to get started on eDofE, you'll play a key role in their development.

Alongside inspiring participants you'll also need to keep a close eye on their progress, assist with any issues through regular meetings and chats and help them to complete their DofE programme.

Recognise and reward achievement

The DofE is all about personal achievement, which is why it's important to recognise every single success of a participant's journey.

As well as verbal encouragement, you may choose to use sectional certificates, which let them know they're a significant step closer to reaching their goals.

See chapter five for more information on sectional certificates.

And, of course, when a participant does achieve their Award, it's essential that their efforts are acknowledged. You and/or your centre may hold presentations and your LO can help you organise high-profile Award presentations to give your participants the recognition they deserve.

Keep in touch

As a DofE Leader, it's important to be aware of how participants are getting on with their programme. If someone isn't attending as regularly as they normally would, or has stopped using eDofE, get in touch to find out why. They might just need a gentle nudge to get back on track. It's important to think about how they might respond best – a text or email may be far more effective than a phone call or letter!

If a participant moves to a new area, help them make contact with a local DofE centre via an LO so they can complete their programme and achieve their Award.

Our website contains contact information for all LOs throughout the UK – www.DofE.org/takepart

Encourage completion

When young people sign up to do their DofE they do so with an expectation that they will complete it. Whilst we accept that a small number of participants will not see their programme through to the end, it is essential that as many as possible achieve their Award. It is your responsibility as their DofE Leader to help them achieve this.

Maintaining regular contact with your participants will ensure that you pick up if they are straying from their goals and enable you to give them some additional encouragement. Use eDofE and regular meetings to check on how your participants are doing.

See chapter five for hints and tips on how to achieve higher completion rates.

Encourage progression

When a participant has completed one level of their programme and achieved

an Award, it's important that you remind them about the next level and actively encourage them to get started on it.

Maintain standards and keep in touch with developments

As a DofE Leader, you'll enjoy a high degree of autonomy but it's crucial that whatever you do meets our national standards. So please make sure that everything your group does is in accordance with the DofE's, your LO's and your centre's requirements, policies and procedures.

Your Licensed Organisation will have its own health and safety policies and procedures in place so make sure you understand and meet these too.

Through regular contact, news on eDofE, newsletters etc. your centre Co-ordinator and LO's DofE Manager will keep you informed of all relevant matters. You can also find key information on our website and in the Resource Zone in eDofE, where (depending on your role) you can upload documents that other Leaders, helpers and participants in your centre or Licensed Organisation might find useful.

Make sure that you also sign up for your free copy of our magazine for DofE Leaders, e-newsletter and other offers and discounts at **www.DofE.org/subscribe**

Insurance

The Duke of Edinburgh's Award provides limited personal accident insurance cover and Licensed Organisations will also have their own insurance in place to cover any claims against them for injury or damage caused to, or by, young people and adults doing a DofE programme.

In some instances where participants are undertaking an activity not organised by their Licensed Organisation or an Approved Activity Provider (see page 115), parents are responsible for ensuring that health and safety and insurance provisions are met.

In your role as a Leader, you need to ensure that participants (or their parents and carers) are aware of this responsibility. For more information, visit **www.DofE.org/go/insurance**

Keep a firm handle on your group's resources and activities

Maintaining a tight grip on your group's finances is vital for delivering services efficiently. Please stick to your LO's and/or centre's policies and procedures in these matters.

The processing and maintenance of procedures, records and details is vital too. Keep copies of your group's enrolment forms, parental consent forms and activity sheets.

One of your key tasks is to make sure your participants are progressing through their programme and to help them to do this, you need to use eDofE to keep in touch.

Make sure that Programme Planners and evidence are approved, sections are signed off and approved Awards are put forward to your Licensed Organisation in good time.

Remember that in many cases, you can approve lots of things with just a couple of mouse clicks.

Stay in touch with your community

Keep an eye out for activities that your group and participants could become involved with around your community. This will be made easier by promoting The Duke of Edinburgh's Award locally and publicising any newsworthy activities and participant achievements. By raising your profile it's likely that organisations and individuals will start contacting you with offers of help.

Actively seeking sponsors and partners could help your group/centre in its work. This could take the form of equipment donations, event sponsorship, use of facilities, providing additional activities, general support and volunteering opportunities. Again, raising your group's profile can help you in this area.

See chapter six for more ideas on how to get your activities noticed.

> *"You don't need a great deal of specialist resources to get started and once you're in the network, you'll probably find that other DofE groups are happy to share. It's important that you have enough adult support to ensure safety and encourage variety. It's also useful to think ahead – DofE has a habit of growing!"*
> Lister Baynes, DofE helper

Maintain and improve services

We are committed to constantly maintaining and improving our services. To monitor and improve the quality of DofE programmes please find out what your participants think of their own programmes. Encourage them to express their opinions on their Assessor's reports and other pieces of eDofE evidence, peer reviews, one-to-one sessions, group discussions, self-evaluations, and other appropriate methods.

Getting your group started

There are different ways to set up your DofE group and each one has unique considerations. Depending on your situation you'll need to do things slightly differently:

- In an existing DofE centre, where there is a need for another group to meet demand from participants. *Your DofE centre will already be authorised to run the DofE – please talk to your DofE Co-ordinator who will explain how the DofE works, who your LO is, help you set up your* group and ensure that all checks are undertaken.

- A centre where young people already meet, when you want to introduce the DofE to them. *If this is the case, please contact your local Licensed Organisation for authorisation to set up a DofE centre and group(s).*
- You want to set up the DofE in your area and are not based at an existing place where young people meet. *You'll need to contact your local Licensed Organisation for authorisation to set up a DofE centre and group(s) and find a venue.*

If you have any issues or concerns or are unsure who your Licensed Organisation is, please contact your DofE Regional/Country Office – *contact details can be found on page 124.*

Contact details for Licensed Organisations can be found at **www.DofE.org/takepart**

Getting the right location is vital

Your group must be based somewhere easily accessible for all participants, e.g. a school, youth centre, commercial premises or sports centre. Wherever possible, it should be somewhere that young people would like to meet. It must also be in a safe environment – both the meeting place, as well as its immediate surroundings.

While it's not necessary to have access to a full IT suite, the internet will give you instant access to all the information you need. Use of any portable device that can connect to the internet can go a long way.

Getting participants involved

Unless you have a ready-made group you're taking over or lots of young people waiting for someone to lead them, you'll need to get young people interested. You can do this in many ways, depending on your situation. For example, you can organise taster evenings, events and presentations, put up posters, announce it over the school loudspeaker system or intranet, or on your youth group's blog or social networking pages.

Existing Award holders are often happy to give first-hand accounts of their experiences – it's a very successful way of attracting new young people. It's also well worth encouraging local businesses to talk about how achieving an Award can benefit a young person's CV. You can also use the local press, radio and the internet to promote your DofE group.

See chapter six for more ideas on generating publicity.

Don't forget – the DofE is open to any young person aged 14-24, regardless of background, location or ability.

Please read our full Equal Opportunities policy in chapter six.

Parents, carers and guardians

Parental consent

You'll need parental consent if participants under 18 want to join your group. Your Licensed Organisation will have its own procedures for enrolling participants which may include the completion of an enrolment or registration form. Participants need to provide an email address on registration so that information can be sent to them to set up their eDofE account.

As the DofE Leader, you must ensure that parents, carers and guardians are always kept fully informed regarding their child's DofE activities.

How parents, carers and guardians can make a difference

The support of parents, carers and guardians can make a big difference to a young person's experience of the programme. It's important that they encourage their children and acknowledge their achievements at every stage.

As it opens the door to unique experiences, achieving an Award often brings young people and their parents, carers and guardians closer together. So be sure to encourage involvement in their children's activities – be it by simply voicing their approval, driving them around or encouraging them to keep going.

Parents, carers and guardians can also be a great help to your DofE group/centre. From assisting with admin or driving minibuses to training or fundraising, there's so much they could do. As their children are involved it's quite likely that they'd be interested in lending a hand, so encourage them to volunteer in any way they can.

"The DofE really is for anyone. My daughter has made so many new friends and discovered loads of new talents she might not otherwise have realised she had."
Dave Ludlow, parent

Participation fees

To take part in the DofE, participants pay a nominal fee. This fee is their contribution towards the Charity's costs in running their DofE programme and represents a personal commitment adding value to their involvement. The fee represents a very small proportion of the overall cost which is supported by the funds raised by the DofE Charity.

Included in the cost, participants receive:
- A **Welcome Pack**
- An **eDofE account**
- **Limited personal accident insurance**
- An electronic copy of their **Achievement Pack** upon completion of their programme

- A **certificate and badge** upon approved achievement of their Award
- Invitation to a **national Gold Award Presentation** (Gold level only).

The current charge for participation can be seen at *www.DofE.org/go/costs*

Your LO and/or centre may add a small administration fee to this amount and they must explain this clearly to participants. You can choose to do the same or charge a weekly subscription fee to cover any extra costs. If this is the case, you must tell the young person and their parent/carer/guardian how much has been added and what it is for.

As the DofE Leader, it is your responsibility to collect and pass each participant's fee to your DofE Co-ordinator/LO. In some centres, the Co-ordinator may handle this for all groups. Once your LO has received it, they will send your participant's *Welcome Pack*, making them officially DofE participants.

Welcome Packs

Once a participant has paid their fee, they will receive a DofE *Welcome Pack* containing information and advice on the DofE and their programme as well as plenty of information to get them started on eDofE and their DofE journey.

eDofE

The next step is for you (or someone in your Licensed Organisation) to set up their eDofE account.

The participant should provide their email address so that they can be sent their eDofE sign in details. They will then receive a welcome email with information on how to get started.

Some of the information that eDofE captures is mandatory, like a participant's personal details or the start and finish dates for each section.

As their Leader you should encourage them to upload photographs and other evidence (although they don't have to) in order to put together a really good *Achievement Pack* (see page 18). They should be reminded what a fantastic record their *Achievement Pack* will be of their DofE journey and how valuable it can be in evidencing to others what they did to achieve their Award.

Whilst photos and other evidence are not a compulsory element to achieve an Award, a participant's eDofE record does need an Assessor's report before the section can be approved by you as being completed.

This Assessor's report is an important mark of quality in a DofE programme, in effect being a written statement from an independent person that shows what a young person has achieved.

When a participant has completed all sections for their current level, you simply use eDofE to submit the Award for approval by your Licensed Organisation.

If at first a participant doesn't achieve a particular section, the Assessor should discuss the reasons with them and only make their Assessor's report once they have successfully completed it.

There are a number of resources available to help get you and your groups started on eDofE.

Check out our website and the eDofE Resource Zone for more information: **www.DofE.org/downloads**

Achievement Pack

The *Achievement Pack* is an innovative and colourful way for participants to record their achievements. It lets them create a lasting memory of their DofE experience.

Participants can create their *Achievement Pack* when they've completed their DofE programme and have achieved their Award. The *Achievement Pack* gives participants the opportunity to upload the best of their evidence from eDofE into a professionally produced publication. So, whether it's 'that' picture from the expedition or a glowing Assessor report, it can be recorded for posterity.

The *Achievement Pack* is a great resource for participants to show potential future employers what they achieved, as well as being ideal for keeping on the coffee table at

home to show off to family and friends. There are two professionally printed versions of the *Achievement Pack* available for purchase or participants can create their own free PDF version, the cost of which is included in their initial Participation Place fee.

Making participation affordable

It is usually programme activities, rather than the cost of enrolment, that can make the greatest financial demands on participants. Encouraging them to devise a programme that matches their resources is all part of the challenge. However, more costly activities can be attainable and many participants organise fundraising events for special activities.

Some grant giving bodies will provide funds and many companies sponsor young people's activities. Additionally, participants may have access to certain equipment through your centre or LO. So if they do have ambitious plans there's still every chance of realising them, they'll just need to be resourceful!

The Handbook for *DofE* Leaders

Helpers

Building your team of voluntary helpers

Groups do what they do thanks to their team of helpers. As a DofE Leader you may also be in charge of recruitment, training and management of the team.

It's important that you take a hands-on role in this area. Always look for individuals who share your interest in helping young people. It's important that they are appropriate to work with young people, have a passion for our work and know how to connect with current and potential participants.

Get to know a helper's individual skills. Then you'll be more able to give them roles that best fit their talents and the needs of your group. From minibus drivers and admin support to activity leaders and Assessors, there are countless ways for people to get involved. It's definitely a case of 'the more the merrier'.

Some helpers might be particularly interested in supporting one area of DofE programmes and may choose to purely focus their efforts on that section. This is a great way to recruit enthusiastic helpers who can support participants in completing their sections.

Don't forget the people who can't commit to turning up every week. They could help in many other ways. For example, there's fundraising for your group's/centre's activities, making the teas on an open day or running a presentation skills training session for your group before their expedition. Just think creatively!

"Helping out with DofE participants is such a rewarding thing to do. It's great to watch their progression and see their confidence grow. Often, when they start out, they know nothing of the skill and aren't confident in their abilities but when they complete their finished pieces you can see the sense of pride in what they've achieved."
Rob Young, DofE Assessor

Above and beyond recruitment and management of helpers, you'll also build relationships with key supporters – from senior staff in your centre to funders and your community. Keep them up-to-date with the developments and requirements of your group.

More specialist support

As a DofE Leader you can't be there every minute of every day for every participant throughout the entirety of their programme. That's why when participants select an activity they need to ensure that they have a suitable Assessor in place, plus potentially a Supervisor as well.

These are not mutually exclusive roles. One person can do one or all of them. And, in certain situations and sections, you may find that you are best placed to take on all of these roles.

Before working with your group, anyone involved in supervising and assessing participants must be checked and approved by your LO as suitably experienced or qualified.

Remember, if the participant is arranging their own activity, then their parents/carers/guardians are responsible for checking safeguarding arrangements but you as their Leader or your centre's Co-ordinator should check the Assessor's experience/qualifications.

Furthermore, prior to helping your participants it's crucial that helpers are fully briefed regarding their roles and responsibilities. Make sure they understand the details of participants' programmes.
You may need to organise extra training to bring helpers up to speed.

Our guides to each section for Leaders and helpers (see **www.DofEshop.org**) are also really useful for someone who's only going to be helping with just one section.

Assessors

An Assessor checks on a young person's progress and agrees the completion of a section of their programme.

They will produce or sign off the relevant Assessor's report for that section, which is uploaded into eDofE.

An Assessor can be anyone who is interested in helping a young person to achieve, has some knowledge of the activity they are doing and can be available over the time they're doing it.

From the local football club coach to a charity shop manager, from the neighbour who's a web designer to the conservation expert leading a residential week, just about anyone can be an Assessor for the Volunteering, Physical, Skills and Residential sections.

However, to maintain the integrity and value of Duke of Edinburgh's Awards, they must be independent. Therefore, they cannot be a family member of a participant.

Because of the nature of expeditions, there are slightly different rules in place for Expedition Assessors – *please see page 84 for full information.*

If you are struggling to find Assessors, talk to your centre's DofE Co-ordinator and/or LO's DofE Manager – many of whom will have contacts and lists of people that have been an Assessor before.

The Assessor should have knowledge of the activity being undertaken and be

The Handbook for DofE Leaders

aware of the young person's objectives. They should also be available at key stages throughout the experience in order to assess the participant's contribution and development.

Once a section is complete, the Assessor will meet with the young person to discuss their performance, their experiences and achievements.

The Assessor will also decide whether the participant has met the DofE requirements – that they've demonstrated effort, perseverance, improvement and made progress towards their section goals. This information, along with comments from the Assessor, should be recorded on the Assessor's report.

Assessor's reports can be submitted in a variety of different ways, these include:

- **Online:** at **www.DofE.org/assessor** then follow the instructions.
- **Phone:** on 0203 368 6644.
- **On paper:** using the *Keeping Track* booklet.

In each case, Assessors will need to provide the participant's name, eDofE ID number, DofE level and the section they have assessed.

At the end of each section, as the DofE Leader, you should spend some time with your participant discussing their sectional achievements and helping them to reflect and identify the skills they have learned.

You should help them to think about how the skills and experiences they have gained can help them in the future.

The participant can add their personal reflections to their eDofE account to be included in their *Achievement Pack.*

Supervisors

These are people with a good understanding of a participant's chosen activities.

A Supervisor is essential for the Expedition section as they are responsible for supervising and supporting a team of participants to ensure their safety and well-being whilst they are doing their expedition.

In the case of the Volunteering or Residential sections, a Supervisor will most likely be connected with the organisation/activity the participant intends to work with.

They will help set goals and regularly meet with the young person to check on their progress, address any potential issues and adjust goals.

Please see pages 82 and 84 for the more detailed roles Supervisors and Assessors have for the Expedition section.

So now you have a venue, lots of participants eager to start, helpers keen to support you and the go-ahead from your Licensed Organisation.

Over the next two chapters we'll cover DofE programmes in detail, so you're ready to give your participants all the support and encouragement they need.

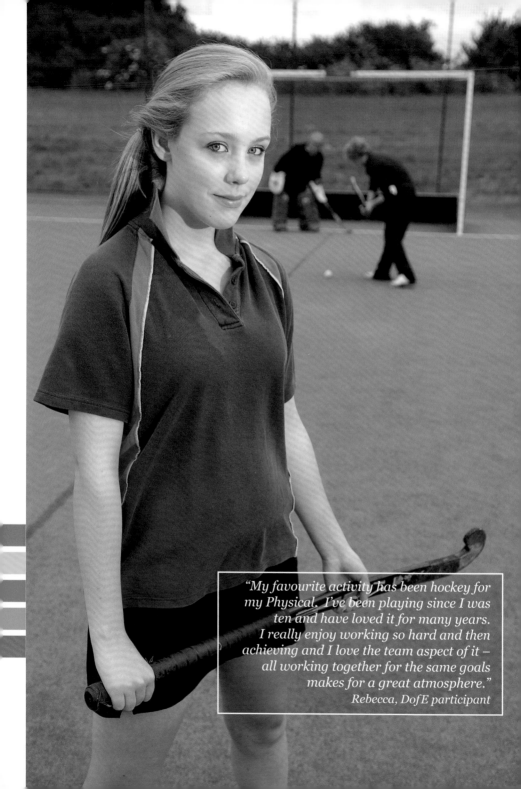

"My favourite activity has been hockey for my Physical. I've been playing since I was ten and have loved it for many years. I really enjoy working so hard and then achieving and I love the team aspect of it – all working together for the same goals makes for a great atmosphere."

Rebecca, DofE participant

Chapter 3
DofE programmes

So what is a DofE programme? How old do participants need to be before they start? What do they need to bear in mind when choosing activities? This chapter will tell you all about the programmes, what they involve and how the process works.

What is a DofE programme?

A DofE programme is the series of activities covering different categories that participants select and undertake to achieve their Bronze, Silver or Gold Duke of Edinburgh's Award. The programme is all about self-development. It's not about being first. It's non-competitive and focuses on helping young people to improve existing skills or gain new talents, abilities or perspectives and being the best they can.

Individual programmes for individual people

Developing initiative is a key part of a participant's involvement. At the start, participants take responsibility for the selection of their own programme. They should consider costs, venue choices, travel requirements and the availability of a suitable Assessor and/or Supervisor. Whilst it is important that participants use their own initiative you will still need to provide support and advice, especially when they're devising their programme and setting objectives.

Remember, though, that you should still allow them a level of flexibility to ensure that their programme remains personal to them.

"The DofE is about trying to help young people help themselves to become well balanced, healthy individuals that have a sense of social and environmental responsibility."
John Hender, DofE Leader

Someone with learning difficulties or limited mobility may take longer to complete a section or require extra training or support. This is not an issue – programmes are designed to be flexible. Remember, this is about young people pushing their own limits.

Though the programmes are an individual challenge there are times when participants will be required to work as a team. In these situations you should provide guidance and ensure that everyone is involved at a level that is appropriate for their development.

With regard to the programmes, the conditions detailed in this *Handbook* must be met, although it is possible to agree variations because of a young person's abilities or location.

At all levels any proposed variations should be discussed with and approved by your centre and LO. At Gold level the appropriate DofE Regional/Country Office must be involved in the consultative process to ensure that participants receive effective guidance based on examples of good practice.

Programme structure

Levels

There are three separate, progressive levels of programmes, which lead to a Bronze, Silver or Gold Duke of Edinburgh's Award. The main differences between them are the minimum length of time required to complete them, the degree of challenge and the minimum age at which young people can start to do them.

"I'm so glad I did my Bronze and Silver before I tried Gold! It gave me a gentle build-up for 'the big one' – especially with the expedition. Much better than 'going in at the deep end'!"
Emma, DofE participant

Bronze, Silver and Gold levels have been created to encourage young people to develop their abilities and progress towards achievement of a Gold Award at a pace roughly commensurate with their age. The required time commitments and progress to be made at each level increases through Bronze, Silver to Gold.

Consideration should be given to abilities of young people as well as their age when introducing them to the DofE. For example, some 17/18 year olds may find it a challenge to achieve a Bronze Award in six months. As their DofE Leader, you need to bear in mind that each level can be a personal challenge for an individual, whatever their age.

Sections

Why do DofE programmes have sections? Each section focuses on developing a core aspect of a young person in a fun yet challenging manner. They have very specific aims and purposes. By doing them all, young people will help their community, develop new skills, confidence, talents and gain a greater appreciation of the world. Achieving an Award really does enrich the mind, body and soul. What's more, every step is an exciting and unique adventure.

Each DofE level has four sections:

- **Volunteering**: undertaking service to individuals or the community.

- **Physical**: improving in an area of sport, dance or fitness activities.

- **Skills**: developing practical and social skills and personal interests.

- **Expedition**: planning, training for and completion of an adventurous journey in the UK or abroad.

- At Gold level, participants must do an additional fifth **Residential** section, which involves staying and working away from home doing a shared activity.

Time and age requirements

Overall requirements

The DofE aims to help young people develop into adulthood. We have therefore established a focus for our activities on young people between the ages of 14 and 25. Within these ages a participant is free to take as long as they wish on their programme, so long as they are under 25 years old when they complete all their activities in their programme.

They are free to work at a pace that they're comfortable with and can achieve their Award.

Our only stipulation is that participants spend the following minimum time doing their programmes.

Please note that, whilst timescales are expressed in months, participants need to give a regular commitment averaging at least an hour a week during this time.

This is because to achieve an Award young people must show persistence, commitment and personal development over a period of time.

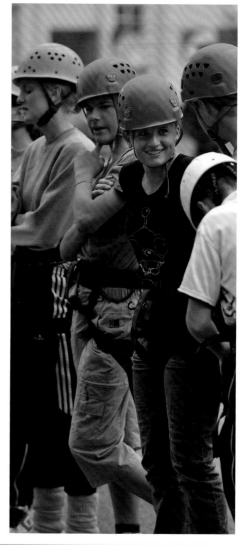

Level	Minimum age they can start	Minimum Length of time	Minimum length of time if they have achieved the previous level
Bronze	14 years	6 months	n/a
Silver	15 years	12 months	6 months
Gold	16 years	18 months	12 months

During their programme they'll need to do each activity for an average of an hour a week over this time. They have until their 25th birthday to complete any programme and achieve an Award.

It's not something that can be achieved through a short burst of enthusiasm one weekend!

Bronze Award (14+ years old)

Three parts of the programme, Volunteering, Physical and Skills, each require a minimum of three months to complete, whilst the Expedition involves planning, training for and undertaking a two-day (one night) expedition.

Participants must also decide whether to spend a further three months on the Volunteering, Physical or Skills section. The decision is entirely theirs. It must be made at the start but can be reviewed later.

It is possible to allow a young person to start their Bronze programme shortly before their 14th birthday, if they are part of a larger group that is aged 14 plus. This often happens when friends or a school year group decide to embark on their adventures together.

However, for this to be allowed, you must be sure that the young person is sufficiently mature to do their programme and also gain approval from your DofE Co-ordinator and Licensed Organisation.

To achieve their Award, participants must have completed their programme and be at least 14½ years old.

Volunteering	Physical	Skills	Expedition
3 months	3 months	3 months	Plan, train for and complete a 2 day, 1 night expedition

*All participants must undertake a **further** 3 months in the Volunteering, Physical or Skills section.*

Silver Award (15+ years old)

Participants spend a minimum of six months volunteering. For the Physical and Skills sections, they must spend a minimum of six months on one and three on the other. The Expedition involves planning, training for and undertaking a three day (two night) expedition.

The decision on which section to do for the longest time is totally theirs. If they have jumped straight into their Silver programme they'll need to do a further six months either volunteering or doing whichever of the physical or skills activity they spent more time on. This decision must be made at the start but can be reviewed later.

To achieve their Award, participants must have completed their programme successfully and be at least 15½ years old if they already have Bronze. Direct entrants must be at least 16 years old before they complete their Silver programme.

LOs sometimes let young people who have achieved their Bronze Award make a start on their Silver Award before their 15th birthday. However, in such situations you must consult with your centre and LO before agreeing anything.

Volunteering	Physical	Skills	Expedition
6 months	One section for 6 months and the other section for 3 months		Plan, train for and complete a 3 day, 2 night expedition
*Direct entrants (i.e. those without a previous level) must undertake a **further** 6 months in the Volunteering or the **longer** of the Physical or Skills sections.*			

The Handbook for D*of*E Leaders

Gold Award (16+ years old)

Participants must be at least 16 years of age to start their DofE programme at Gold level. No activities can count until their 16th birthday.

Participants spend a minimum of 12 months volunteering. For their Physical and Skills sections they must spend a minimum of 12 months on one and six on the other. Again, they decide which section to do for the longer time. They'll plan, train for and complete a four day (three night) expedition. The biggest difference at Gold is that participants must do an additional, fifth section – Residential. This is an activity away from home for five days and four nights with people they do not already know.

Direct entrants must spend a further six months either volunteering or doing whichever of the skills or physical activities they spent the most time on. This decision must be made at the start but can be reviewed later.

To achieve their Award, participants must have completed their programme successfully and be at least 17 years old if they already have their Silver Award. Direct entrants must be at least 17½ when they complete their programme.

You should encourage your participants to continue activities beyond the minimum time requirements of their programme in order to meet their personal ambitions.

Volunteering	Physical	Skills	Expedition	Residential
12 months	One section for 12 months and the other section for 6 months		Plan, train for and complete a 4 day, 3 night expedition	Undertake a shared activity in a residential setting away from home for 5 days and 4 nights
*Direct entrants (i.e. those without a previous level) must undertake a **further** 6 months in either the Volunteering or the **longer** of the Physical or Skills sections.*				

Maximum Age

The upper age limit for the completion of all programmes is a young person's 25th birthday. Extensions to the upper age limit can only be considered when illness, accident or unavoidable circumstances make it impossible to complete a programme by the age of 25. In such situations, your LO must send a written request to your DofE Regional/Country Office. If the application is successful, extra time will be allowed. This must not be exceeded.

When and how young people can do their D*of*E

A DofE programme is all about personal choice and responsibility. Participants do their activities either in their own personal time, partly as one of a range of options in supported/core time or as an after-school programme.

Activities may even take place during school hours or working hours but participants must be able to prove that their activities still required a substantial contribution of personal time and voluntary effort.

The amount of personal time required may need to be reduced when necessary, for example, for young people with additional support needs or where access to the facilities for an activity is constrained (e.g. by availability times or access).

They should not do activities that are entirely curriculum subjects with no extra personal effort. For example, essay writing purely based on A-level assignments is not acceptable but a programme that includes entering a school writing competition could meet the requirements.

Using programme activities as a framework to support or create an alternative curriculum or education programme, e.g. for young people at risk of exclusion, is also allowed, even if it is done in a school environment and entirely in scheduled lesson time.

Choosing activities

There is a massive choice of activities that count towards DofE programmes. Participants can select practically any activity they wish – as long as it's legal and morally acceptable. It could be something that they're currently into or a completely new area.

However, this much choice can be overwhelming, so you need to help participants select activities that they'll really enjoy and set achievable but challenging objectives.

As their Leader, if you're in doubt about any of your participants' activity choices, look at the sectional outcomes and discuss it with your LO before giving your approval for the young person to start their programme.

Achieving a Bronze, Silver or Gold Award is all about personal development and that requires taking responsibility and initiative. From the start, participants must take ownership of their programmes by choosing the activities they wish to pursue in each section.

Activities are placed in specific sections for a reason. When participants are making their choices it's essential that you're on hand to advise them and support them in their decisions.

This is to ensure that any choices meet section aims, principles and benefits as well as the requirements of any DofE programme (see chapter four).

You'll also need to make sure that their choice is available locally (Expedition and Residential sections aside).

Don't panic, we're not expecting you to be an expert in every section! Chapter four will give you more guidance in this area. You do, however, need to be aware of the aims and requirements for each section so you can advise your participants and recruit Assessors and Supervisors for any activity.

As a DofE Leader it's important that you ensure all participants get the most out of their programmes. The best way of doing this is by helping them choose a balanced range of activities.

Encourage participants to spread their wings with their choices – they shouldn't just focus on one area of interest across all the sections. For instance it's great if a participant is playing football and wishes to do this in their Physical section. However, selecting activities for every section except their expedition that focus on football is not a good move for most young people. After all, the aim is to broaden horizons and try new experiences.

Ultimately participants need to choose activities that they are going to enjoy. It could be something that they are already doing or perhaps one they've always wanted to try. There is such a wide choice that whatever they would like to do, the odds are they can.

If you're unsure about a certain activity – whether it's OK to do or simply which section it belongs in – contact your LO who will advise you.

The key when choosing activities is to ignite a participant's imagination. Get them really thinking about things they'd love to try or do. But equally keep their feet firmly planted in the real world. Make sure participants take into consideration their personal circumstances, local availability and potential costs when choosing.

Don't forget that LOs have overall responsibility for monitoring the quality of participants' experiences and safety. They will have additional guidelines relating to particular activities, which you will need to be familiar with and ensure are met.

Chapter four contains more information about the detailed requirements for each section and examples of programmes for each section. More inspiring ideas can also be found at www.DofE.org

Setting a challenging programme

When advising on a programme and objectives always bear in mind what level of expertise the young person already has, their maturity and level of confidence. The goals they set need to be challenging but achievable. If it is too unrealistic, it may in fact damage a young person's confidence and self-belief.

Remember, our aim is to help young people develop themselves. This will only occur if they set realistic challenges.

Once a participant has decided upon their programme, you need to review it before they start, while they're doing it and once they've finished. This is to check they are happy with their progress, the activities selected and that their objectives are challenging enough.

If required, these can always be reset to make them more challenging or achievable.

eDofE is a useful tool to help you to do this. However, it should never replace the face to face interaction between a Leader and a participant.

Activities undertaken prior to entry

One activity done before a young person starts their DofE programme could count towards the achievement of an Award if it was done during the preceding three months.

All activities must have been done in accordance with DofE programme principles, conditions and age requirements.

Taking a break

Although they should ideally progress from Bronze to Silver and then Gold, it's totally up to a participant as to when and what order they do each section within each level. As long as they complete their programme and achieve their Award before their 25th birthday, they are free to take a break for holidays, exams or if they just feel they need a rest.

The process for a DofE programme

Like most things in life, young people get out of a DofE programme what they put in. So to ensure participants get the maximum benefit out of their activities and achieve their Awards, we've devised the process below. Please follow it faithfully.

The process has four key stages that apply to all sections and activities:

> 1: Preparation
> 2: Training
> 3: Activity
> 4: Assessment

Preparation

Participants need to think about and research what they would like to do for each section. They may talk to friends and family about their ideas. It's quite likely your participants will want to talk to you too. Your role during this stage is to support and, if necessary, advise them on their choices.

Once the participant has made their decisions, arrange a meeting with them.

Alternatively ask one of your group's helpers to do this and report back to you. During the meeting discuss the participant's choices and the commitments required. Establish that they have thoroughly researched their selection, are happy with their decisions and cover the following areas:

- **Aim:** what do they want to do/achieve? Discuss the aim and benefits of the section and how that is reflected in the young person's own programme choice.
- **Activity:** do the activities fit their personal objectives and the requirements of the DofE?
- **Details:** think about/suggest final objectives as well as interim goals and milestones. Establish, agree and write down personal goals in the section Programme Planner in eDofE that are practical, measurable, achievable, exciting and have realistic timings.
- **First steps:** is any training required? What about any safety or legal requirements?
- **Recording their journey:** establish a system for how the young person will record their efforts, what evidence you would like to see in eDofE and when you will conduct regular progress reviews.
- Remind them **how their Award is authorised** and the type of celebration they can expect when they finally achieve it *(see chapter five).*

With these items discussed and agreed, your participant can design an individual programme that takes into account their needs along with the principles and requirements of a DofE programme.

In addition to eDofE, Programme Planners are available to help participants create their programme from **www.DofE.org/sections** – there is one for each section.

Training

There will regularly be times when a participant's choice of activity requires them to take a course, simple introduction or structured training before starting their activity. This should be understood and agreed by both the young person and you. Participants should be fully aware of the time, resources and equipment that may be required to undertake their training.

In the Physical and Skills sections the activity may be training to achieve their goal, for example, to gain a qualification such as a sports award or music grade (respectively).

In the Volunteering section, training can count towards the time requirements as long as it is in proportion and the aim of the section is clearly achieved. Volunteering must be based around practical help to the community not just training in a skill that may help the community in the future.

See the sectional information in chapter four for more clarification.

Activity

This is often the most important and enjoyable part of any section – the actual doing bit! As a DofE Leader you need to be constantly supporting and encouraging your participants.

Meet with them regularly to talk about how they're getting on, help them to add evidence to eDofE and sort out any problems they may be facing. These discussions will enable you to adjust programmes or goals and address any additional training or general needs that could assist their progress.

Assessment

To complete a DofE programme every activity undertaken must be successfully completed and assessed. So when the time comes to review your participant's efforts their Assessor (which may be you), you as their Leader or one of your helpers must meet them to discuss:

- The goals that were set and what the participant actually achieved.
- What challenges were faced and how they were overcome.
- The overall experience and what they enjoyed.

The meeting also provides the perfect opportunity to celebrate the young person's achievements. It is also the ideal time to encourage them to complete their other sections, achieve their Award and progress to the next level.

Remember to ensure that the Assessor, you and your participants have completed the relevant Assessor's report and that this has been uploaded into eDofE.

These key stages are covered in more detail in chapter four, including the differences between each section.

Changing activities

If absolutely necessary, activities may be changed once in each section at each level. However, we would not encourage this as participants will not gain the full benefit of developing their skills and knowledge of their activities.

If a participant does need to change then they must restart the preparation, training, activity and assessment process.

The timescale for the second activity will be shorter, as the two activities together will need to add up to the minimum overall time requirements for that section/level. When this occurs both activities must be recorded in their eDofE account but you as their Leader must authorise this.

Authorisation of Awards

A participant has achieved a Bronze or Silver Award when the Licensed Organisation confirms that all relevant conditions have been met, based on the information recorded in the participant's eDofE account.

At Gold, if not completed on eDofE, a Gold Award notification form (available at **www.DofE.org/gold**) must be completed and signed by the participant and you as their DofE Leader. This must then be given to your centre's Co-ordinator, who will send it to your Licensed Organisation.

They will then check and forward it to the appropriate DofE Regional/Country Office for final confirmation.

Starting the next level

Participants should be encouraged to complete their entire programme to achieve their Award before embarking on the next level. However, they may start on a section of the next level prior to completing the previous one if they:

- Have reached the minimum age of entry for the next level.
- Have completed that section of the previous Award and had it approved by the Leader.
- Are not working on all three levels at the same time.

eDofE is a powerful tool to help you monitor your participants' progression and encourage completion.

Please refer to chapter five for more information on completion, recognition and progression.

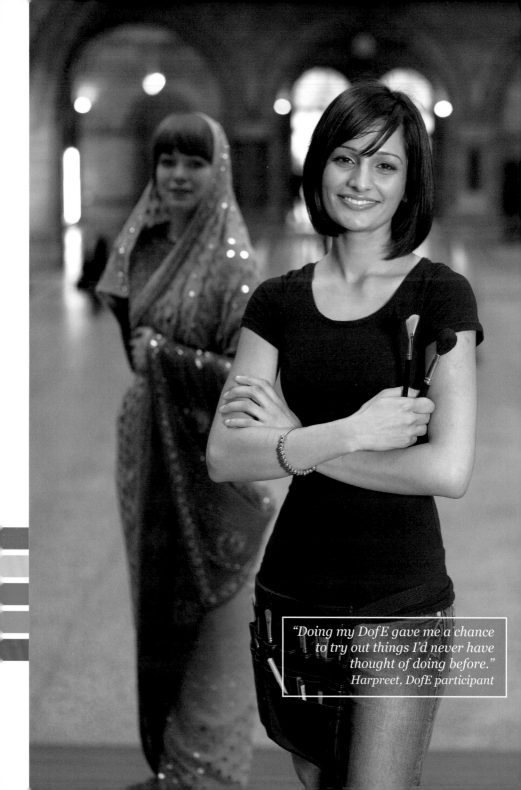

"Doing my DofE gave me a chance to try out things I'd never have thought of doing before."
Harpreet, DofE participant

Chapter 4

The sections in detail

This chapter will take you through the sections of a DofE programme in greater detail. From selecting activities, to training, doing and successful completion, this chapter gives you the information you need to deliver a fulfilling and exciting experience for all your participants.

Your responsibilities as participants undertake their sections

As a DofE Leader, you will be expected to:

- Inspire young people to achieve their full potential.

- Help young people choose activities based on their interests, the needs of the community and personal circumstances.

- Ensure that your participants' programmes remain personal to them.

- Motivate them to either create their own or take part in existing activities.

- Inspire young people to complete their programme and achieve their Duke of Edinburgh's Award.

- Help them to stay safe.

- Give them the knowledge, understanding or training needed to participate and get the most from their DofE programme.

- Help young people to complete their DofE programme using eDofE.

- Help them find a suitable Assessor and/or Supervisor as required to help them during their activities. The person(s) selected must have a full understanding of the activity the participant is pursuing and a desire to help young people achieve.

- Help them set appropriate and challenging personal goals for each activity.

- Make sure they put any training into practice.

- Encourage full commitment throughout their DofE programme.

- Encourage them to move on to the next level.

The Handbook for DofE Leaders

The right choices for the right sections

As a DofE Leader it is important that you ensure participants select the right activities for the right sections. This can be confusing and the differences may seem marginal, but making the wrong selection will ultimately mean that a young person cannot complete their programme and achieve their Award.

For instance, learning first aid is a skill but spending time as a first aider is a volunteering activity as it involves helping others. Equally, dance is a physical activity but dance appreciation would be classed as a skills activity because it is about learning theory rather than physical performance.

As their Leader, you are responsible for checking that young people's choices count towards the correct sections. All activities must fit into one of the sections. Guidance notes are available on **www.DofE.org/sections** and in the Resource Zone on eDofE. If at any time you are unsure about an activity, please consult your LO.

Timescales and dates

The minimum time requirements for every section at each level can be found in chapter three.

The start date for each section should be the date of your first preparation meeting, and the finish date is when the activity has been completed, assessed and recorded on the participant's eDofE account.

Volunteering

■ Volunteering

Aim

To inspire young people to make a difference within their communities or to an individual's life and develop compassion by giving service to others. From DJing at the local hospital to assisting at an animal shelter, from renovating a heritage site to coaching sports at a youth club – the options are almost limitless.

Principles

- People have a responsibility to each other. By volunteering, communities are improved and strengthened.
- Young people are passionate about many things and should be encouraged to make a positive contribution to something they care about.
- The commitment to volunteering should be recognised; therefore young people are rewarded for this activity with the completion of a section of their DofE programme.

Benefits

Through volunteering, participants:
- Learn about their communities and feel a sense of belonging and purpose.
- Learn to take responsibility for their communities and their own actions by committing and persevering with an activity.
- Build new relationships with members of their community, decreasing fears and prejudice and increasing community cohesion.
- Get a chance to develop teamwork and leadership skills, increasing their employability and work experience.
- Further understand their own strengths and weaknesses by evaluating their own progress and building confidence and self-esteem.
- Have the opportunity to trust others and in turn be trusted.
- Enjoy new adventures.

What is required?

Volunteering is simple. It's about choosing to give time to do something useful, without getting paid for their time (apart from expenses). It can be helping people, the community or society, the environment or animals. Volunteering must not be done for a business but can be undertaken for a charity or not-for-profit organisation.

Team volunteering

We know the benefits of doing an activity in a team are significant for young people. Therefore, why not encourage young people to identify a local need, plan how to meet it and then do their volunteering together? Team volunteering may also be ideal for young people who cannot find an appropriate individual opportunity, especially if they are under 16.

An example of this could be a youth group that is concerned that their local playground is covered in graffiti and litter. Together they develop an action plan. Doing it will see them dealing with their local council and police as well as talking to local businesses about sponsoring the play equipment and bins. They can then clean up the playground with the appropriate tools and celebrate the changes and their achievements in the local paper.

More support can be found at
www.DofE.org/leaders

This flowchart gives a simple overview of the steps involved for a young person to complete their Volunteering section. Each step is explained in more detail on the following pages.

Preparation
Young people plan their volunteering experience and set their objectives on eDofE. This includes who/what they will help, what they will do, where they will do it and how long for.

↓

Training
Participants undergo any training necessary to allow them to undertake their practical volunteering activities (no more than a quarter of the overall time).

↓

Activity
Participants do their practical volunteering activity regularly, averaging at least an hour a week, for the planned time.

↓

Assessment
The young person meets with their Assessor to discuss and record their experiences, how they developed and reached their goals. and updates their eDofE account.

The Handbook for *DofE* Leaders

The four steps to completing the Volunteering section

1. Preparation is everything

Before starting their volunteering activity participants must thoroughly research the charity, organisation or people they are helping and have an Assessor willing to support them. Their Assessor will usually be an adult in the organisation with whom the young person is volunteering, often their named contact. For team volunteering this is likely to be you.

A participant's research and understanding of who they're helping will enable them to develop goals that are achievable yet challenging. As DofE Leader you, or a nominated helper, should make sure that they set them with their activity Assessor and that their achievements will lead to some form of personal development. Ensure a participant's activity is focussed on skills and experience, as well as meeting the needs of others or the environment. Their volunteering activity could be individual, team or DofE group based.

2. Training may be required

The young person may require some training before starting their activity

and some organisations have training courses that must be done before volunteering can start. If possible, any training undertaken should result in accreditation or a qualification. Furthermore, it should take place towards the beginning of the time period and take up no more than a quarter of the overall time.

Timescales: Volunteering

Level	Minimum time	Notes
Bronze	3 or 6 months	*Young people must do one of their Volunteering, Physical or Skills sections for 6 months, the others for 3.*
Silver	6 or 12 months	*Young people who haven't achieved Bronze must extend their Volunteering or the longer of their Physical or Skills sections to 12 months.*
Gold	12 or 18 months	*Young people who haven't achieved Silver must extend their Volunteering or the longer of their Physical or Skills sections to 18 months.*

Remember, young people must commit to regular activities averaging at least an hour a week during this time.

For example, a first aid course lasting three months would not be a suitable volunteering activity for a Bronze Award (this would be a skill). However, it is in proportion and acceptable for a Gold participant who then volunteers for St. John Ambulance for another nine months.

Volunteering must be based around practical help to the community not just training in a skill that may benefit the community in the future.

Remember, many training courses that don't count for the Volunteering section may well be acceptable as a Skills section activity if a participant wants to do it.

3. Activity – time to start volunteering!

With the research done, goals set and any required training successfully completed, your participant is ready to begin their volunteering activity.

They will need to commit their personal time to doing unpaid work which benefits the environment, a community, organisation or individual.

The bulk of their time should be spent actually doing the work required, such as digging out the canal, leading skateboarding at an after-school club, community leadership by taking an active role in a local youth council or assisting with the local shopmobility

The Handbook for *DofE* Leaders

scheme. They may also need to attend relevant meetings, prepare resources or help to organise an event.

4. Assessment – completing the section

At this stage the participant meets their Assessor to discuss and record their experiences, how they developed and reached their goals.

As their DofE Leader you should help to organise this meeting or you may be doing this role yourself.

Additional areas that will need discussing and recording in the participant's eDofE profile are:

- Positive experiences and adventures they had along the way.
- How they felt at the beginning and the end.
- What they gained from it personally (think soft skills like teamwork, communication, planning).

- Any difficulties they faced and how they overcame them.
- What impact they feel they had on their communities.

Don't forget that an Assessor's report must be uploaded to the participant's eDofE account to prove they have successfully completed this part of their programme.

At the end of each section, as the DofE Leader, you should spend some time with your participant discussing their achievements and helping them to reflect and identify the skills, knowledge and understanding they have acquired whilst undertaking this section.

What can young people volunteer to do?

The list of types of volunteering and examples of activities shown overleaf should help you to point participants in the right direction when they're selecting their volunteering activity. Remember, activities can be undertaken on an individual or group basis.

*Guidance notes are available from **www.DofE.org/volunteering** and in the eDofE Resource Zone.*

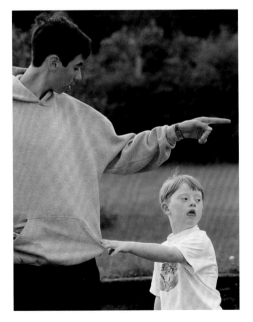

Volunteering section ideas

For this section, participants need to identify a need which they wish to help with and then see which of the categories below it fits into. They then need to plan what they can do to help and create their programme to meet this need.

Listed in each category are examples of programmes that participants could do.

Helping people
Examples:
- Supporting a local primary school with their reading scheme.
- Being a DJ in their local youth club.
- Being a weekly visitor to an older person.
- Being a Listener for the Samaritans in a prison.
- Helping at an after-school club for children with cerebral palsy.

Community action and raising awareness
Examples:
- Running a web campaign for their college to raise awareness of the issues around poverty in the world.
- Being an active member of Streetcred, the Youth Opportunities and Capital Fund for Bedfordshire.
- Running a campaign in their local faith group reminding people to register as an organ donor.
- Running a crime prevention project in their school with the local police.
- Being an active member of a youth council or forum.

Coaching, teaching and leadership
Examples:
- Being a DofE Leader.
- Being a uniformed youth group leader.
- Teaching numeracy to year six pupils.
- Being a football coach.
- Helping to coach their school's swimming team.

Working with the environment or animals

Examples:

- Helping with a local canal conservation project.
- Running a recycling project in their ATC Squadron.
- Doing a litter picking project for a local housing estate or park.
- Helping at a Cats Protection adoption centre.
- Running a campaign to stop people wasting energy.

Helping a charity or community organisation

Examples:

- Raising money for a cancer charity by organising a fashion show.
- Working in a charity shop.
- Being a trustee for a local charity.
- Helping with religious education classes.
- Decorating/doing up their Sea Cadet Unit's Headquarters.

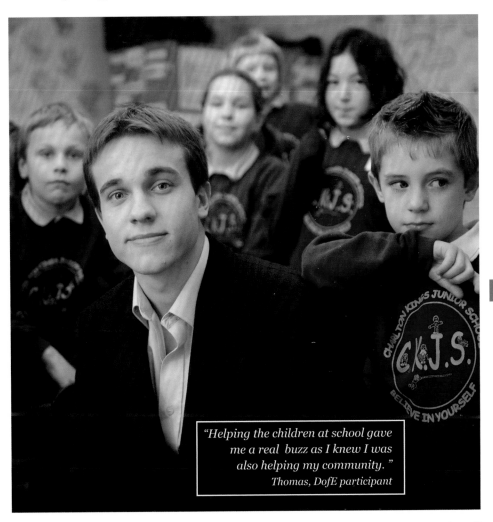

"Helping the children at school gave me a real buzz as I knew I was also helping my community."
Thomas, DofE participant

Physical

Physical

Aim

To inspire young people to achieve greater physical fitness and a healthy lifestyle through participation and improvement in physical activity. From hockey to dance, rock climbing to swimming, wheelchair basketball to yoga – almost any dance, sport or fitness activity can count.

Principles

- Involvement in some form of enjoyable physical activity is essential for young people's physical health.
- Maintaining physical health is important to mental and emotional well-being.
- A lasting sense of achievement and satisfaction is derived from meeting a physical challenge.
- Physical activities are enjoyable in themselves and can lead to the establishment of a lasting, active lifestyle.

Benefits

Through doing physical activities, young people will:
- Have fun keeping fit by choosing an activity which they enjoy.
- Improve fitness by taking part in a physical activity on a regular basis.
- Discover new abilities.
- Raise self-esteem through improvement of performance.
- Extend personal goals by involvement and sustained interest.
- Set and respond to a challenge by extending physical fitness and performance.
- Experience a sense of achievement from meeting a physical challenge.

So what is a physical activity?

In short, anything that requires a sustained level of physical energy and involves doing an activity. For example, playing a sport regularly and showing personal improvement would count. However, learning to become a coach in the same sport would be a Skills section activity, whilst being a volunteer coach counts for the Volunteering section.

Participants must choose a physical activity and with your help set an appropriate challenge. They can choose one they are currently doing or go for something new. The key is to show progression and sustained interest over time. Ultimately, participants must prove that they have broadened their understanding and increased their expertise in their chosen activity.

If your participant is unsure which category an activity falls into, or whether it's acceptable, they must get approval from you, your DofE Co-ordinator and your LO before starting. Generally this will be relatively straightforward if the activity has a national governing body or if it is recognised by UK Sport, the Central Council of Physical Recreation or the relevant Sports Council.

Helping young people to make the right choice

They don't need to be an Olympic athlete, pro-footballer or prima ballerina to achieve in the Physical section.

This flowchart gives a simple overview of the steps involved for a young person to complete their Physical section. Each step is explained in more detail on the following pages.

Preparation
Young people plan their physical activity and set their objectives on eDofE.
This includes what sport, dance or fitness activity they want to do,
where they'll do it and for how long.

↓

Training
Participants undergo any training or briefing necessary
to allow them to undertake their physical activities.
Training may form part of the activity.

↓

Activity
Participants do their physical activity regularly, averaging
at least an hour a week, for the planned time.

↓

Assessment
The young person meets with their Assessor, to discuss and record their
experiences, including their effort, perseverance and achievement.
and updates their eDofE account.

The Handbook for *DofE* Leaders

The key here is to have fun and become better and fitter. From wheelchair users who've learnt to scuba dive to nervous teenagers who've joined an aerobics class, from inner-city young women who've set up their own football team to young offenders who've built self-esteem through gym work – achievement is possible regardless of a young person's starting point or physical ability.

As a DofE Leader you must ensure that a participant's choice:
- Focuses on one specific theme or activity.
- Enables Assessors to easily measure progression over a period of time.
- Is undertaken in accordance with appropriate safe working practices and legal requirements.
- Is usually done in their own time.
- Reflects their individual interests, talents and capabilities.

Participants are free to do this section independently or as part of a team. To help set a 'benchmark' for monitoring and assessing progress, encourage them to go for a national governing body standard or award where appropriate.

The four steps to completing the Physical section

1. Preparation is everything

During their first meeting with you, or a nominated helper, the young person must agree their activity and set objectives. These should be tailored to their level of experience in the activity. This meeting must cover:
- What they plan to do, i.e. the practical activity, commitment required and its benefits.
- The starting point for the participant, recognising their current knowledge and personal ability.
- The agreed programme incorporating individual goals and ambitions.
- Any necessary safety or legal requirements.
- Whether they require support or training related to health and safety, skills and awareness.
- The process for evaluation and assessment, *see step four*.
- How progress is to be recorded and the format of the final review.
- The dates and times of meetings.

They then complete their Programme Planner on eDofE.

Timescales: Physical		
Level	Minimum time	Notes
Bronze	3 or 6 months	*Young people must do one of their Volunteering, Physical or Skills sections for 6 months, the others for 3.*
Silver	3, 6 or 12 months	*Either the Physical or Skills section must be done for 6 months, the other for 3. Young people who haven't achieved Bronze must extend their Volunteering or the longer of their Physical or Skills sections to 12 months.*
Gold	6, 12 or 18 months	*Either the Physical or Skills section must be done for 12 months, the other for 6. Young people who haven't achieved Silver must extend their Volunteering or the longer of their Physical or Skills sections to 18 months.*

Remember, young people must commit to regular activities averaging at least an hour a week during this time.

2. Training to develop their talents

In order to complete this section a participant may have to undertake some form of training or briefing, prior to starting or even during their activity. It could be one of their sectional objectives or, equally importantly, a health and safety requirement.

3. Activity, enabling physical talents to bloom

With the goals set, participants can get going with their chosen activity. On a regular basis they should meet with you, their Supervisor and/or their Assessor to:

- Discuss progress
- Obtain clarification and guidance
- Obtain help to resolve any problems
- Reflect on progress and learn from experience
- Reaffirm or set new goals and discuss expectations for the next phase
- If necessary, review their choice of activity.

4. Assessment, completing the section

A participant's effort, perseverance and achievement should be regularly assessed throughout their time on this

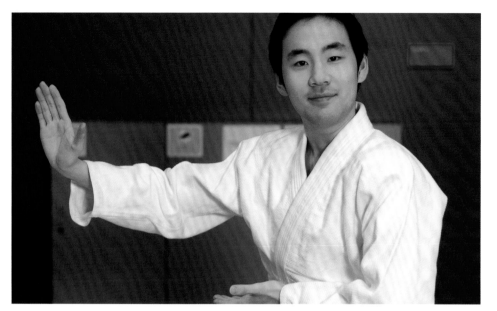

section. If applicable, their contribution to the planning, execution and completion of their team's activities and performance must also be examined.

Participants have completed this section when their Assessor is happy that:
- The minimum time requirements have been met.
- Genuine effort and individual progress have been made within the young person's capability.

Your participant, together with their Assessor, will discuss and record their experiences in eDofE, along with:
- How they developed and achieved their goals.
- The difficulties they faced and how they overcame them.
- Their contribution to their team or group.

Other areas that should be considered and recorded in the participant's eDofE profile during this final review are:

- Effort
- Application
- Technique
- Skill
- Tactics
- Improvement in fitness and achievement
- Knowledge of the relevant rules and safety regulations
- Quality of experience.

Don't forget an Assessor's report must be uploaded to the participant's eDofE account to prove they have successfully completed their programme.

At the end of each section, as the DofE Leader, you should spend some time with your participant discussing their achievements and helping them to reflect and identify the skills, knowledge and understanding they have acquired whilst undertaking this section.

Guidance notes are available from **www.DofE.org/physical** *or from the Resource Zone in eDofE.*

Physical section ideas

For this section, participants need to identify a physical activity that they want to get involved in, or improve at, from any of the categories below. They then need to set themselves objectives and create their programme to meet them. Listed in each category are examples of programmes that participants could do.

Team sports
Examples:
- Joining a local football team and playing in matches regularly.
- Taking part in after-school hockey lessons.
- Learning the rules of ultimate flying disc and joining their college team.
- Joining their Girls' Brigade Company's netball team and playing in their league.
- Playing wheelchair basketball at their school.

Individual sports
Examples:
- Joining a local athletics club and competing for their area.

- Setting regular dates to go bowling with a group of friends.
- Learning to fence at a local community centre.
- Learning to horse ride at the local stables.
- Practicing trampolining every week and joining in a local competition.

Water sports
Examples:
- Learning to windsurf at a local lake.
- Gaining a PADI open water SCUBA diving qualification and going out on subsequent dives.
- Joining a local dragon boat racing team and competing at a regatta.
- Going swimming every week at the local pool.
- Learning to surf on holiday and continuing to practice at their local beach.

Racquet sports
Examples:
- Learning to play tennis in their lunchtime club at school.
- Playing badminton every week with friends.

The Handbook for *DofE* Leaders

- Playing table tennis regularly at their youth club.
- Joining a tennis club and playing in matches.
- Having squash lessons at their local gym.

Dance

Examples:

- Learning bhangra at a local dance studio.
- Attending salsa classes every week at the local community centre.
- Creating a street dance routine with friends for their District Scout Gang Show.
- Improving their ballet skills and gaining the next grade.
- Joining, and performing with, a local sword dancing team.

Fitness

Examples:

- Going to their local gym every week and improving cardiovascular fitness.

- Jogging or walking every week with friends.
- Doing an activity class, e.g. aerobics, pilates, yoga, at their local sports centre.
- Playing golf and improving their handicap.
- Learning to weightlift in a prison gym and showing improvement.

Extreme sports

Examples:

- Mountain biking with friends and learning how to do jumps.
- Skateboarding regularly at their local skatepark.
- Joining a free running group.
- Improving their climbing ability at the local climbing wall.
- Learning how to skydive and doing two tandem jumps.

Martial arts

Examples:

- Improving their karate skills and gaining the next belt.
- Taking part in self-defence lessons at an after-school club.
- Joining tai-chi classes in their local park.
- Learning the skills of Capoeira at local classes.
- Joining a judo club at their local community centre.

Skills

■ Skills

Aim

To inspire young people to develop practical and social skills and personal interests. From podcasting to playing a musical instrument, fine art to website design, cookery to learning to drive, the sky's the limit!

Principles

- By choosing to develop a particular skill young people realise their unique potential and gain greater self-esteem.
- Everyone has the ability to learn. Young people should have the opportunity to develop skills.
- All young people have unique potential and should value themselves. Developing a skill will help them realise this.

Benefits

By learning a skill, participants will:
- Develop a new talent.
- Improve self-esteem and confidence.
- Develop practical and social skills — by working alongside enthusiastic individuals who share their skills and knowledge.
- Develop better organisational and time management skills.
- Sharpen research skills — by using libraries, the internet and the local community, they will have to identify and source help and guidance.
- Learn how to set and rise to a challenge.

Something old or something new – selecting a skill

Participants must choose an activity and, with your help, set an appropriate challenge. They can choose to develop a new skill or improve an existing one. The key is to show progression and sustained interest over time.

Ultimately, participants must be able to prove that they have broadened their understanding and increased their expertise of their chosen skill. Activities can be undertaken on either an individual or group basis.

Most DofE groups/centres are only able to offer a small selection of activities that count as a skill. If a young person wishes to try something else they can organise it themselves and check the details with you for approval. This must be done before they start.

Helping young people to make the right choice

As a DofE Leader you must ensure that a participant's choice:
- Focuses on one specific theme or activity.
- Enables their Assessor to easily measure progression over a period of time.
- Is undertaken in accordance with appropriate safe working practices and legal requirements.
- Is normally done in their own time.
- Reflects their individual interests, talents and capabilities.

While all sports require skill to play, this does not mean that they can be used for the Skills section. Some participants may like to focus on the skills theory and the history of a sport for their Skills section.

However, as this is often part of a Physical section programme anyway, their skills activity must be carefully constructed to meet the outcomes of the Skills section and agreed in advance with you.

This flowchart gives a simple overview of the steps involved for a young person to complete their Skills section. Each step is explained in more detail on the following pages.

Preparation
Young people choose to improve an existing skill or develop a new one. They research their choice, plan what to do, how long for and set their objectives on eDofE.

Training
Participants undergo any training necessary to allow them to undertake their skills activity. The skill chosen could be a course, in which case training will be the full activity.

Activity
Participants undertake their skills activity – learning by doing regularly, averaging at least an hour a week, for the planned time.

Assessment
The young person meets with their Assessor to discuss their experiences, what they learned and how they met their goals and records it all in their eDofE account.

The Handbook for DofE Leaders

- The starting point for the participant, recognising their current knowledge and personal ability.
- The agreed programme incorporating individual goals and ambitions.
- Any necessary safety or legal requirements.
- Support or training related to health and safety, skills and awareness.
- How progress is to be recorded and the format of the final review.
- The dates and times of meetings.

The four steps to completing the Skills section

1. Preparation is everything

It's vital that the participant researches their chosen activity thoroughly prior to meeting with you to discuss their choice. This will enable them to discuss constructively what personal goals should be set. During the meeting you must cover:
- The process for evaluation and assessment.
- The activity to be pursued i.e. the practical task, commitment required and the benefits to the participant.

The start date for this section is your meeting and the finish date will be when the skill has been fully assessed and recorded on eDofE.

2. Training to develop their talents

Development of a skill is often a combination of training and practical activity. For some activities, initial training may be required so that young people are safe to do the work, whereas for others, the skill chosen could be a course and it will be the full activity. If this is the case, it is likely that the adult doing their training will also be their Assessor.

Timescales: Skills

Level	Minimum time	Notes
Bronze	3 or 6 months	*Young people must do one of their Volunteering, Physical or Skills sections for 6 months, the others for 3.*
Silver	3, 6 or 12 months	*Either the Physical or Skills section must be done for 6 months, the other for 3. Young people who haven't achieved Bronze must extend their Volunteering or the longer of their Physical or Skills sections to 12 months.*
Gold	6, 12 or 18 months	*Either the Physical or Skills section must be done for 12 months, the other for 6. Young people who haven't achieved Silver must extend their Volunteering or the longer of their Physical or Skills sections to 18 months.*

Remember, young people must commit to regular activities averaging at least an hour a week during this time.

3. Activity, enabling talents to bloom

Participants learn by doing their programme. Therefore ongoing support through meetings with you, their Assessor and/or Supervisor is crucial. During these meetings it is important to:

- Discuss progress
- Clarify and provide guidance
- Help to resolve any problems
- Reflect on progress and learn from experience
- Reaffirm or set new goals and discuss expectations for the next phase
- If necessary, review the choice of activity.

4. Assessment, completing the section

All participants should be regularly assessed to check their effort, perseverance and achievement. Their contribution to the planning, execution and completion of group activities will also fall under the spotlight.

Participants have completed this section when their Assessor is happy that:

- The skill has been regularly followed for the required time.
- Genuine effort and individual progress have been made within the young person's capability.

Your participant, together with their Assessor, will discuss and record their experiences in eDofE, along with:

- How they developed and their progress towards achieving the objectives they set.
- Difficulties faced and how they overcame them.

Don't forget that an Assessor's report must be uploaded to the participant's eDofE account to prove they have successfully completed this part of their programme.

At the end of each section, as the DofE Leader, you should spend some time with your participant discussing their achievements and helping them to reflect and identify the skills, knowledge and understanding they have acquired whilst undertaking this section.

*Guidance notes are available to download at **www.DofE.org/skills***

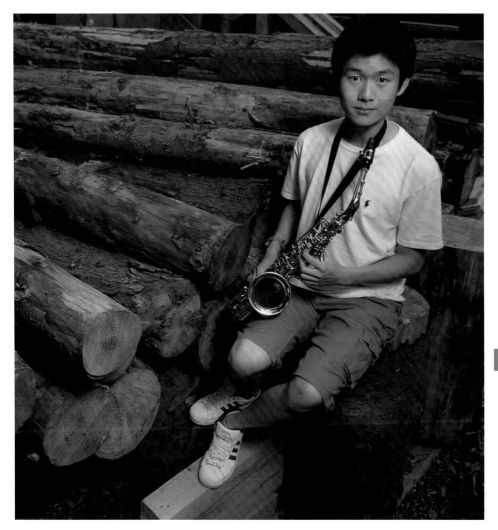

Skills section ideas

For this section, participants need to identify a skills activity that they want to learn, or improve at, from any of the categories below. They then need to set themselves objectives and create their programme to meet them. Listed in each category are examples of programmes that participants could do.

Creative arts
Examples:
- Learning how to knit and making a piece of clothing.
- Researching and learning a variety of interior design techniques and putting them into practice.
- Learning how to make spun sugar and decorating their own pastries for a competition.
- Doing art classes at a local centre and taking part in an exhibition.
- Developing woodworking skills and learning how to build benches for their local public space.

Performance arts
Examples:
- Going to speech drama classes at a local club.
- Creating a comedy sketch show, filming it and putting it online.
- Singing in a school musical.
- Learning a variety of circus skills including juggling and magic tricks to perform at a children's party.
- Pulling together a flashmob group at school and creating a range of routines.

Science and technology
Examples:
- Designing and building a free app for a smartphone.
- Taking part in an after-school experimental science club.
- Joining a local astronomy club.
- Teaching themselves to create and manage their own website.
- Designing and building elastic band-powered aircraft.

Care of animals
Examples:
- Taking their dog to obedience classes.
- Feeding animals at their local farm and learning key handling skills.
- Mucking out horses and learning how to care for them.
- Learning about and keeping tropical fish.
- Helping a local beekeeper at the weekends and tasting the honey created.

Music
Examples:
- Learning to DJ and playing at friends' parties.
- Taking piano lessons and gaining a higher grade.

- Playing the drums in a band with their mates and holding a gig for family and friends.
- Joining the school choir.
- Studying classical music and attending concerts.

Life skills
Examples:
- Learning how to cook food from different countries at their local youth group.
- Undertaking a first aid course with their St. John Ambulance Group.
- Learning how to drive and being able to demonstrate basic car maintenance.
- Learning about interview and CV-writing techniques with a local business.
- Being an active member of a Young Enterprise group at their college.

Learning and collecting
Examples:
- Learning about their family tree and giving a presentation to their youth group.
- Collecting old comics from various sources and researching their history and development.
- Learning about aircraft recognition and attending air shows to improve their knowledge.
- Studying geology and collecting different rock types.
- Compiling a book on the fashion and style icons of the last decade.

Media and communication
Examples:
- Learning about today's digital lifestyle, creating a video clip and posting it online.

- Learning British Sign Language.
- Taking a writing course and publishing an article in the Boys' Brigade magazine.
- Joining their university debating society.
- Producing and distributing a newsletter for their youth group.

Natural world
Examples:
- Studying orchids and successfully growing a selection.
- Maintaining a pond in their garden and studying pond life.
- Growing vegetables on an allotment and entering them in the village fete.
- Learning about conservation and environmental work through after-school classes.
- Studying groundsmanship by shadowing a local groundskeeper at a football club.

Games and sports
Examples:
- Joining a local snooker club and playing in the league.
- Taking part in an after-school chess club.
- Being taught how to fish on a local river by a family friend.
- Learning how to go-kart at a local track.
- Working to achieve an ATC Regional Marksman Award.

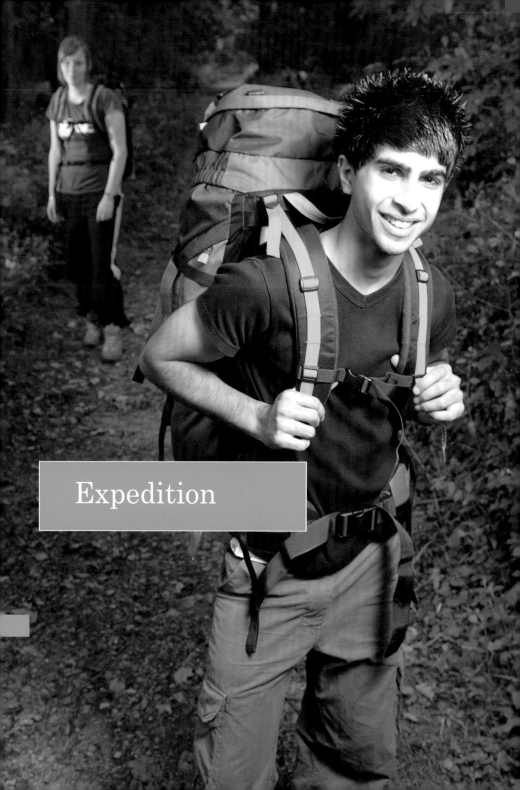

Expedition

◼ Expedition

Aim

To inspire young people to develop initiative and a spirit of adventure and discovery, by planning, training for and completing an adventurous self-sufficient journey as part of a team. From cycling in the Galloway Hills, walking in the Brecon Beacons or canoeing down the Thames to sailing in the Mediterranean, horse riding in Chile or walking in the Atlas Mountains, participants choose where and how they want to undertake their expedition.

Principles

- Participation in shared experiences in the outdoor environment can develop initiative, teamwork, communication, leadership, problem solving and organisational skills.
- Experiencing and overcoming challenges together develops emotional strength and empathy for others.
- Working with a team of peers in the outdoors, experiencing isolation and solitude develops self-reliance and self-confidence.

Benefits

Through participation in an expedition young people:
- Gain an appreciation of and respect for the outdoor environment.
- Learn the value of sharing responsibility for success, through leadership, teamwork, self-reliance and co-operation.
- Learn the importance of attention to detail and organisational ability.

- Develop and demonstrate enterprise and imagination.
- Become more self-reliant.
- Become more able to overcome both expected and unexpected challenges.
- Recognise the needs and strengths of themselves and others.
- Improve decision-making skills and the ability to accept consequences.
- Gain the skills to reflect on personal performance.
- Learn to manage risk.
- Learn through experience.
- Develop perseverance and determination.

What is involved?

The Expedition section involves planning, training for and completing an unaccompanied, self-reliant expedition with an agreed aim.

All participants must have appropriate training, do at least one practice expedition in the UK, complete a qualifying expedition (the one that is assessed) and deliver a presentation in order to complete the section.

Expeditions must be completed by the participants' own physical efforts with minimal external intervention and without motorised assistance.

This flowchart gives a simple overview of the steps involved for a young person to complete their Expedition section. Each step is explained in more detail on the following pages.

Preparation
Participants plan an expedition. This includes team members, its aim, how they will travel and the environment they intend to travel through. Expeditions may be undertaken by foot, bicycle, sailing boat, canoe, kayak, wheelchair or on horseback.

↓

Training
Participants undergo training in expedition skills and their chosen mode of travel.

↓

Practice expedition
Participants must undertake sufficient practice expeditions to enable them to travel safely and complete their qualifying expedition.

↓

Qualifying expedition, debrief and presentation
Once prepared, participants undertake their expedition, which will be observed by their Accredited Assessor. On completion they will be debriefed by their Assessor and then prepare and give a presentation, in any medium, of their expedition which covers their aims, experiences and outcomes.

↓

Assessment
The Accredited Assessor should provide their report for eDofE following the qualifying expedition and reports should also be provided by a person who saw their presentation.

This *Handbook* sets out the rules and conditions of the Expedition section. Leaders must refer to the *Expedition Guide* for further information and clarification about this section.

The five steps to completing the Expedition section

1: Preparation is everything

First, participants should decide on their expedition team. There must be between four and seven young people in a team (eight for modes of travel which can be used by two people at once, e.g. tandem bikes, open canoes). Many DofE groups will have more participants than the number required for just one team and you may need to help them work out who will be in each team. Teams can be chosen in many ways: friendship groups, shared choice of aim/location or skills in a particular mode of travel etc.

If a participant is struggling to find a group to join for their expedition (either because they are an independent participant or perhaps their school group etc is full), they could join an open expedition (see page 84). Details of open expedition opportunities can be found at www.DofE.org/opportunities

Members of the team should have a similar level of experience and ability. The DofE is open to all and every participant will have different strengths and weaknesses so the planning should take this into account.

With teams in place, young people need to decide on the nature of the expedition that they wish to undertake. They must first consider what they want their aim to be, then the location and mode of travel. The expedition's aim should relate to the interests and abilities of those taking part and the area they will be travelling through. This is the key to any expedition's success. Without it, they can't plan an effective, challenging expedition with a clear outcome – simply travelling through the countryside is not enough. Some examples of aims could include:

- A piece of work related to the environment they're travelling through, for example, examining footpath erosion or studying the local wildlife.
- Monitoring and evidencing the impact of a physically demanding expedition on the body by walking all day and measuring calorie intake, heart rate and pulse compared to normal.
- Using canoes to explore and research historical buildings on a lake system.
- Examining group dynamics and teamworking.

The expedition aim and format must be agreed in advance of the qualifying expedition with the DofE Leader and Supervisor, but may be altered if circumstances change.

Gaining an understanding of the local culture of an area is vital to any trip, particularly outside the UK, but the isolation aspect of the section means

that this cannot be an expedition aim. Any research, for example visiting a museum; must be done in the acclimatisation period or after the expedition.

It is worth reminding your participants at this time that their post-qualifying expedition presentation will be based on this aim so it must allow for their own observations and investigations during their expedition.

Once their aim is set, it will guide their choice of an appropriate environment in which to do their expedition. It will also provide a guide as to the amount of time a team will spend journeying or exploring.

Finally, working with you and/or their Supervisor, the team should choose their mode of travel. This should be suitable for the aim and location, something they have the skills to do (or will learn to do) and that they will find enjoyable. With all this in place, you can agree with your team(s) their training plan and dates of practice and qualifying expeditions.

2: Training to develop their knowledge

Safety is paramount when it comes to the expedition. Therefore, it is essential that participants undertake expedition skills training using the DofE's Expedition Training Framework.

This provides a structure for training young people undertaking their Expedition section. Using it can help prepare young people to meet the challenges of their expedition.

There are additional guidelines to assist with specific modes of travel, such as the paddle expeditions document, available at **www.DofE.org/expedition**

The Expedition Training Framework covers:
- First aid and emergency procedures
- An awareness of risk and health and safety issues
- Navigation and route planning
- Campcraft, equipment and hygiene
- Food and cooking
- Countryside, Highway and Water Sports Codes (as appropriate)
- Observation and recording
- Team building
- Proficiency in the mode of travel.

You can read the detailed Expedition Training Framework in the *Expedition Guide,* in the Resource Zone on eDofE and at **www.DofE.org/expedition**

EX^2 (our interactive expedition training tool) also contains further details along with practical advice and training support. This is available from our shop at **www.DofEshop.org**

3: Practice expedition(s)

Both enjoyable and essential, practice expedition(s) must replicate as closely as possible the conditions of the actual expedition. This includes equivalent daily hours of journeying, mode of travel, accommodation and terrain.

Participants must complete at least one UK practice expedition at each level. This must include sufficient experience of being unaccompanied and remotely

supervised so the Supervisor can confidently sign off their ability to undertake an unaccompanied qualifying expedition.

The Supervisor must be satisfied before the start of the qualifying expedition that the participants have the expedition skills and fitness levels appropriate for the qualifying expedition they are about to undertake.

Never forget that you and their Supervisor must be confident that they will be able to safely complete their qualifying expedition unaccompanied. As their Supervisor gains greater confidence in the team's abilities, they can reduce their level of close supervision enabling the team to undertake unaccompanied journeys prior to going on the qualifying expedition.

If you (the Leader) are not the Supervisor, you should keep in regular contact with them to ensure you are happy with their progress.

At Bronze level a minimum one day and overnight practice expedition is required. Silver and Gold practices must include at least two days and two nights away, consecutively.

Any team undertaking a qualifying expedition in a wild country area must have completed a practice expedition of the appropriate duration (see above) in a wild country area.

The last practice expedition should not be immediately before the qualifying expedition, as time is needed for reflection and recovery.

4: Activity, qualifying expedition and debrief

The team should plan how they will spend their time to complete their expedition and meet their aim.

It is crucial that the speed of journeying, the distance travelled and the time spent exploring is determined by the team to meet their individual needs. Experienced DofE Leaders and Supervisors will enable young people to choose a sufficiently challenging combination of journeying and exploring. This should be based on their experiences during practice expeditions in a similar environment.

A good team can work out average distances based on their training and practice expeditions.

Time associated with overnight accommodation and catering is additional to the minimum daytime hours of planned activity.

eDofE Mapping
eDofE Mapping is a free expedition route submission tool designed to create standard DofE route cards and route summaries. It can be used by anyone using eDofE and helps speed up the route approval process.

eDofE Mapping allows participants and Leaders to produce digital files that can be printed, emailed, saved or uploaded onto eDofE as evidence. However, as stated on page 71 for safety reasons, while on expedition, teams must carry full OS maps or appropriate charts with them and not rely on eDofE Mapping print outs.

Timescales for qualifying expeditions

Level	Duration	Minimum hours of planned activity each day
Bronze	2 days and 1 night	At least 6 hours during the daytime (at least 3 of which must be spent journeying)
Silver	3 days and 2 nights	At least 7 hours during the daytime (at least 3½ of which must be spent journeying)
Gold	4 days and 3 nights	At least 8 hours during the daytime (at least 4 of which must be spent journeying)

Time associated with overnight accommodation and catering is additional to the minimum daytime hours of planned activity.

Recommended environments

General requirements	
Land environment (walking, cycling and horse riding)	All expeditions should avoid villages and populated areas unless that is impossible. Long distance footpaths should not be used, particularly by Silver and Gold teams, except in small sections to link up other paths or areas outside of the UK where they are the only routes available. Teams should not aim for more than 500m of height gain or descent on any one day although cycling expeditions may climb more.
Canoeing and rowing	Local access agreements must be checked in advance for all expeditions.
Sailing	Practice and qualifying expeditions should take place in different areas. Where this is not practical, different routes over the same area can be used.

Bronze*	
Land environment (walking, cycling and horse riding)	Normal rural countryside which can be familiar and local to the participants.
Canoeing and rowing	Canals, rivers or other inland waterways and lakes.
Sailing	Inland waters or sheltered estuaries well within the participants' competencies.

Silver*	
Land environment (walking, cycling and horse riding)	Normal rural, open countryside or forest, which is unfamiliar to the participants. The environment should be more demanding for participants than at Bronze level. Where possible the expedition should all be in, or at least include, areas of open country or forest.
Canoeing and rowing	Canals, rivers or other inland waterways and lakes in rural areas.
Sailing	Inland waters, estuaries or sheltered coastal waters.

Gold	
Land environment (walking, cycling and horse riding)	Wild country** (remote from habitation) which is unfamiliar to participants. The environment should be more demanding for participants than at Silver level. Remote estuaries, marshes, fens and coastal areas may provide an appropriate environment for an expedition with the emphasis on exploring rather than journeying.
Canoeing and rowing	Rivers or other inland waterways and lakes in rural areas, sheltered coastal waters or estuaries.
Sailing	Inland waters, estuaries or sheltered coastal waters. Yachts may be used in open sea areas.

Bronze and Silver teams who plan expeditions in surroundings more demanding than those recommended must be trained and equipped to enable them to meet any potential hazards. The DofE Expedition Training Framework for the appropriate environment should be used. Teams should consider how they will continue to progress their expedition challenge at subsequent levels.
**Wild country is defined as an area remote from habitation. DofE expeditions should be through, rather than over, wild country – it's all about solitude not altitude.*

For a map of UK wild country areas see **www.DofE.org/go/expeditionareas**

Each area has an Assessor Network Co-ordinator and a group of experienced helpers able to assess teams and provide local expedition advice. The contact details of all Expedition Co-ordinators are available from **www.DofE.org/go/expeditionareas**

Equipment
Teams should carry all their equipment and food to enable them to operate in a self-sufficient way. However, there may be some cases when a participant has circumstances that make it inappropriate for them to carry full camping and cooking equipment and it cannot be carried by the rest of the team. In these cases only, some items may be deposited at the camp sites or agreed check points. This must be agreed between the LO and Assessor.

Each individual must carry the personal emergency equipment as listed on our website. Equipment should be checked by the Supervisor for its suitability before the start of the expedition.

Specific equipment guidance
- **Maps and compasses:** Every UK expedition team must take with them full OS maps or appropriate charts for the area(s) in which the expedition is being undertaken. All teams undertaking a DofE expedition should have with them sufficient compasses, route cards and maps to allow for effective navigation and to ensure the safety of all participants should the team split up for any reason. All teams should plan alternative poor weather routes.
- **First aid kits:** Each DofE participant should carry their own first aid kit

with them on expedition rather than, or in addition to, a communal kit for the whole team.

- **Mobile phones:** Using mobile phones on expedition can destroy the sense of isolation and solitude core to the learning and self-reliance of this section. While useful additional safety tools, and in many cases a useful means of capturing evidence, the DofE strongly recommends that mobile phones be used for emergencies only. The expedition team, Supervisor and Assessor should agree in advance the policy of use during their expedition, for example, their use as a camera to record evidence for eDofE and not as a means of communication. Mobile phones must always be considered an unreliable safety tool due to possible lack of reception etc.
- **GPS:** The increasing sophistication of GPS and handheld mapping devices make them a good additional safety tool for DofE groups. DofE groups may use GPS devices as a secondary navigation tool, but there must be no reduction in the syllabus or quality of the navigation training and competency of the team. The expedition team, Supervisor and Assessor should agree in advance the policy of use during their expedition.
- **Personal music players:** DofE teams can take personal music devices with them on expedition but they should not be used during hours of activity and especially when journeying. The expedition team, Supervisor and Assessor should agree in advance the policy of use during their expedition.

Accommodation

The route should be a continuous journey and participants should stop at different locations each night. A camp site may only be used more than once when necessary to meet their aim. Teams should still travel to and from the camp site as part of their journeying.

Lightweight camping enhances the sense of adventure and self-reliance. However, on rare occasions to take into account the needs of participants, alternative basic types of accommodation may be considered.

Preparing for a wild country expedition

Wild country expeditions are exciting and rewarding but it's essential that the team is fully prepared for the environment and know how to use their equipment. Teams intending to travel through wild country areas must ensure that the appropriate Assessor Network Co-ordinator has been notified. Route notifications must include alternative, low level (lower risk) routes that can be used in the event of poor weather.

Teams who would like to use a Network Assessor will need to book and pay for these services in advance of the expedition. Information about the process for expedition notifications and booking Assessors can be found at **www.DofE.org/expedition** or through your Licensed Organisation.

For expeditions in wild country, participants should always arrive the day before the start of their qualifying expedition. This way the entire team and the Supervisor can meet the Assessor and make an early start. At Gold, the team must set aside an acclimatisation day before the expedition in order to get used to the environment. Supervisors can use this time to check local access and complete any additional practical risk assessments. This also provides the team with an opportunity to do research for their aim and experience the local environment.

To enhance the experience, the base camp site should not be used by the team as an expedition camp site.

5. Assessment and evidence

Qualifying expeditions must be assessed by an Accredited Assessor (see page 84). During the expedition the Assessor will meet with the team at various times to check on progress.

Debrief

Whilst the team will be excited and very tired, make sure the Assessor conducts a full debrief immediately after the expedition is completed (on the final day). During this meeting everyone in the team should participate in reviewing the outcomes of the expedition. After the debrief it is important to give participants time to reflect on their expedition and its aims. This will enable the team to prepare and deliver a presentation of their experiences.

Following the qualifying expedition and debrief, the Assessor provides a report that participants can use in eDofE. Participants then give a presentation to their chosen adult to complete the section. This adult then provides evidence that the presentation has been completed which can be uploaded to eDofE. Participants should be encouraged to add their own comments of their experience into eDofE.

Presentation

It is entirely up to the team how their presentation is delivered – it could be in any format. This should be decided on in advance of the expedition and can be completed as a team or as individuals. With your agreement, they can choose who they want to present it to. It could be you, their Supervisor, their Assessor or another suitable adult.

It is usual for the person chosen to know the team and their individual abilities. The presentation must reflect the aim of the expedition and represent a genuine effort and contribution from all members of the team.

Participants on open expeditions may want to deliver their presentation soon after their expedition is completed but time must be allowed for them to collate their thoughts and findings so that the presentation is a distinct event separate from the expedition de-brief. The presentation should also include an account of the journey to encourage participants to reflect on their experiences.

Recording the Expedition section on eDofE

As the Expedition section is a team activity, both Leaders and participants are able to record training, practice journeys, qualifying expeditions and presentation details, as well as other evidence into eDofE. Leaders are able to do this for the whole team at the same time and the Leader entries do not need further approval.

All participants must still enter their own personal aim and goals for their qualifying expedition before the section can be approved.

The 20 conditions of the Expedition section

	DofE qualifying expedition conditions	Further explanation and interpretation of conditions
1	All expeditions must be by the participants' own physical effort, without motorised or outside assistance.	Motorised wheelchairs may be used where appropriate to the needs of the participant.
2	All expeditions must be unaccompanied and self-sufficient.	a) The team must be unaccompanied, unguided and supervision must be carried out remotely. b) As part of effective remote supervision, teams may be more closely supervised for parts of the expedition where specific hazardous areas are unavoidable. This supervision should be kept to an absolute minimum. c) If a team does not possess the necessary physical, first aid and expedition skills required for an area, then they should not be in that area.
3	All expeditions must be supervised by an adult who is able to accept responsibility for the safety of the team.	
4	The expedition must have an aim.	
5	All participants must be properly equipped.	
6	Participants must have completed the required training and practice expeditions.	The qualifying expedition must not be over the same route or in the immediate vicinity of routes used in practice expeditions.
7	At least one practice expedition must be undertaken at each level of the programme, in the same mode of travel in a similar environment to the qualifying expedition.	For overseas assessed expeditions, at least one UK practice must have taken place in an appropriate environment.
8	The team must plan and organise the expedition.	Multiple teams should not travel in convoy but have individual routes from camp site to camp site. Where this is absolutely unavoidable at least 30 minutes must separate each team using the same route and they must operate as discrete teams.
9	Assessment must be by an approved Accredited Assessor.	
10	There must be between four and seven in a team (eight for modes of travel which have tandem).	Unless in the event of an emergency, the team must always keep together.

The Handbook for DofE Leaders

11	All participants must be within the qualifying age of the programme level.	This is regardless of whether they are under assessment or not.
12	Participants must be at the same level of assessment.	Participants should have a similar ability or level of experience and must make a full contribution to the team.
13	The team must not include those who have completed the same or higher level expedition.	Participants should have a similar ability or level of experience and must make a full contribution to the team.
14	Accommodation should be by camping.	See page 72 for further details.
15	The expedition must be of the correct duration.	a) The expedition must be of the minimum number of days and nights and must include appropriate acclimatisation/final preparation time. b) An acclimatisation day during an expedition due to extreme altitude may be included as long as the minimum hours of activity and journeying are still completed. c) An additional acclimatisation/rest day may be included during an expedition but this will not count toward the expedition days.
16	The expedition should normally take place between the end of March and the end of October.	The expedition must take place at an appropriate time of year for the expedition's location and aim and the enjoyment of the participants.
17	The expedition should take place in the recommended environment.	The expedition should take place in an appropriate and challenging environment. At Silver and Gold levels this must be unfamiliar to the participants. Overseas expeditions should take place in an area appropriate to the level of the expedition.
18	The expedition must meet the minimum hours of planned activity.	a) Six hours at Bronze, seven hours at Silver and eight hours at Gold. At least half of these daily hours must be spent travelling. b) Time associated with overnight accommodation and catering is additional to the minimum daytime hours of planned activity. c) Reasonable time for lunch and other appropriate breaks can be included within the hours of planned activity.
19	A substantial meal should be cooked and eaten by participants each day.	This is optional on the final day.
20	A presentation must be prepared and delivered after the expedition.	The presentation or report, which may be in any format the participants or teams choose, must be related to the expedition's aim.

Variations to the 20 conditions

Where participants have individual needs that mean one or more of the 20 conditions cannot be met, they may apply for a variation to enable them to complete their DofE expedition.

Variation application forms and guidance on how to apply are available on the eDofE Resource Zone and at **www.DofE.org/expedition** or from your Licensed Organisation. Variation forms must be approved at the appropriate level. Always get advice from your LO before submitting a variation form.

Variations should be requested at the earliest opportunity, particularly for overseas expeditions, and be submitted in sufficient time to reach the relevant office at least 12 weeks prior to the date of departure. Written approval of these variations should be included in the appropriate notification process to help the Assessor.

Advice and guidance for expeditions with groups with additional support needs can be found on the eDofE Resource Zone, in the DofE *Expedition Guide* and at **www.DofE.org/expedition**.

Multiple teams

Some large DofE centres may have several expedition teams being assessed in the same area at the same time. The DofE strongly discourages multiple teams using the same expedition route as teams should plan their own journey. Multiple teams must always operate independently and discreetly. Where the use of the same route is absolutely unavoidable, usually due to the expedition environment, for example canoe expeditions, rather than the availability of Supervisors, then the teams must be separated by at least 30 minutes journeying time.

Expeditions outside the United Kingdom

Expeditions outside of the UK provide varied challenges which can inspire and broaden young people's experiences. All Expedition section conditions apply equally to expeditions taking place outside the United Kingdom.

Information about the process for expeditions outside the UK can be found at **www.DofE.org/expedition** or through your Licensed Organisation.

The expedition provider, whether this is you or an organisation you have brought in to help, must accept responsibility for monitoring the safety of the expedition. This must be done in accordance with the policies and guidelines of your Licensed Organisation.

If accepted by your LO, your DofE Regional/Country Office will provide you with a notification reference number, which must be entered in the participants' eDofE record on successful completion of the expedition.

In some cases for overseas DofE expeditions, the cost of taking an additional person to be the Assessor can be prohibitive so there is some flexibility in these instances.

For overseas expeditions it is acceptable for the Supervisor to also take on the role of Assessor, if they are accredited by the DofE, while support staff such as teachers or helpers manage the pastoral care of the team.

Even in cases where the Supervisor may have been involved in the team's training programme this is acceptable. If it is possible for an independent person to be the Assessor then this option should always be used as best practice. The team must agree this in advance with their Licensed Organisation.

The team should notify the destination country's National Award Authority, if the International Award operates in that country. For contact details visit **www.intaward.org**

Something else...

The Expedition section aims to inspire young people to develop initiative and a spirit of adventure and discovery. The DofE encourages and will always consider innovative and creative expedition proposals from participants even if they do not meet all of the 20 conditions.

To request approval from the DofE send a written expedition proposal to the DofE Head Office for consideration. These proposals will be one-off expeditions in the UK or overseas and can only be used by participants over the age of 16 for any DofE level.

Some conditions, such as the need for the team to be unaccompanied or for an appropriate practice expedition to be completed, are not flexible but other conditions may have some flexibility.

Participants should seek the guidance of their DofE Manager at least six months prior to the expedition and before they have committed to any expenditure. Send the proposal to the DofE at least 12 weeks prior to the date of departure. The DofE will issue a notification number for participants to enter into their eDofE record on successful completion.

Note: In giving approval for such expeditions, The Duke of Edinburgh's Award only confirms that the expedition complies with the aim, principles and purpose of the Expedition section. We do not accept responsibility for health and safety or public liability insurance.

Other modes of travel

The DofE encourages participants at all levels to be adventurous and consider modes of travel for their expedition other than going on foot. Changing modes of travel as they progress from level to level can add interest and broaden horizons while being part of the challenge of progression.

Other modes of travel for DofE groups are cycling, canoe or kayak, rowing, horseback and sailing including dinghies, yachts or multihull and sail training vessels. However groups have also completed expeditions on other modes including camels, dog sled and skis.

To facilitate and encourage these other modes of travel the DofE provides

specific conditions and advice to support their delivery. Participants need to be competent in the skills set out in the DofE Expedition Training Framework, both for the DofE level and mode of travel.

The DofE strongly recommends that teams considering other modes of travel purchase the DofE *Expedition Guide* which sets out in much more detail advice and guidance for undertaking such expeditions.

Horseback expeditions
Hours per day:
Preparing to travel each day when using horses takes time, feeding, tacking up and so on; more time is needed at the end of the journeying too. At Bronze level up to an hour of the minimum planned activity time can be allocated to do this and up to two hours at Silver and Gold levels. The minimum hours of journeying at each level must still be achieved (three at Bronze, three and a half at Silver and four at Gold).

Practice expeditions:
Both rider and animal must be prepared for the challenge of the qualifying expedition. It is likely that groups will complete more than one practice expedition, for example one on foot and one on horseback. This helps to ensure that they are competent and confident in the skills needed for the DofE level and expedition area, particularly if in Wild Country.

The need for these practices will depend on the experience of both participants and the horses. These practices may be in the same area each time.

Pre-positioned equipment:

Expedition teams must always be independent and self-sufficient, however horses can only carry so much weight, both rider and equipment. Horseback teams may pre-position some of their equipment which is over the load bearing capacity of the animal on expedition.

Pre-positioned equipment must be of the same lightweight type that would have been used if travelling on foot. Participant camping equipment and food may be pre-positioned at campsites, but emergency equipment, the days food and sleeping bags must always be carried.

Items associated with the essential well-being of the horse must be carried each day; however fodder and haynets, grooming tools and rug, spare namnahs and girths and water and feeding buckets may be pre-positioned at camp sites.

Paddle and rowing expeditions

Group size:

For tandem canoes/kayaks or craft designed for multiple occupancy the maximum team size is eight, otherwise seven as with other modes of travel.

Training:

The nature of paddle expeditions is such that the minimum training requirements for all expeditions is the Silver Expedition Training Framework and mode of travel requirements. Some areas will require all elements of the Gold framework. Expedition Training Framework documents are available at **www.DofE.org/expedition**. All participants must also know the rules of conduct for the water on which they are journeying.

Planning:

The water used for Silver and Gold levels must be unfamiliar to the participants but teams may reconnoitre the route beforehand from the bank.

Supervision:

For all paddle expeditions the Supervisor must be in the area of the expedition.

Rivers and canals: The sense of isolation and solitude experienced during an expedition is one of the essential experiences to meet the outcomes for the section. Accordingly, it should not usually be necessary for Supervisors to shadow teams on the water.

If the Supervisor feels that this is necessary then it may be that the team is not sufficiently well trained for the chosen environment. However, as highlighted in condition 2b of the 20 conditions, Supervisors can shadow the team on the water where specific, hazardous areas are unavoidable.

Estuaries and coastal waters: For teams in sheltered estuaries or sheltered coastal waters Supervisors must provide safety cover afloat. Contact should not be made with the team during the expedition except for the needs of supervision. The safety cover must be sufficiently remote from the participants to avoid destroying the team's sense of remoteness and self-sufficiency and yet able to render assistance in an emergency within a reasonable amount of time. The safety cover may consist of shadowing the team from an appropriate distance.

Sailing:
Sailing expeditions can provide

participants at all levels the opportunity to develop themselves and learn a range of new skills.

The wide variety of vessels and numerous flexibilities allowed for these modes of travel are set out against the standard 20 conditions.

Please see page 74 for the full 20 conditions.

Condition	Dinghy variations	Yacht/multihull variations	Sail training vessel variations
1	No outboard motors to be used.	Motors may be used when appropriate including in harbours, berths and when good seamanship and safety dictates. Motors may also be used when there is a lack of wind in order to maintain the spirit of adventure and personal development of the expedition.	
2	Staff may not be aboard the participant's vessels. The team may be accompanied by a safety boat.	Staff may be aboard the vessel. The Supervisor and Assessor should not be involved in the skippering, crewing, navigation, control or management of the boat, except in an emergency for reasons of safety. Regular contact with coastguards should be put in place.	
3	The Supervisor must have appropriate qualifications, relevant to environment and the mode of travel. If the Supervisor is an Accredited Assessor then they may be both the Assessor and Supervisor. Thus minimising adult intervention.		

The Handbook for D*of*E Leaders

Condition	Dinghy variations	Yacht/multihull variations	Sail training vessel variations
6	Participants should be appropriately trained, using the RYA training framework as a reference and have completed the Expedition Training Framework for the appropriate DofE level and environment.	Participants must be competent at the mode of travel to complete their expedition and reference could be made to the RYA cruising syllabus. Week-long experiences that include training and a final expedition may be considered by the DofE on a case by case basis. Acclimatisation is essential at all levels in anticipation of seasickness. Ideally, practice and qualifying expeditions should take place in different areas, where this is not practical, different routes over the same area can be used.	
	Participants must have completed the Expedition Training Framework for the appropriate DofE level and mode of travel. Ideally, practice and qualifying expeditions should take place in different areas, where this is not practical, different routes over the same area can be used.		
8	Participants must be able to demonstrate the ability to passage plan their expedition. However, dynamic planning will always be a feature of all sailing expeditions.		
9	Where expeditions take place in inland waters, lakes, lochs and sheltered estuaries, the Supervisor should, where safe and practical, accompany the expedition in another vessel. For expeditions on sheltered coastal waters and open sea areas the Assessor should be aboard the vessel and hold relevant qualifications. Where Accredited Assessors hold the relevant qualifications and are approved by the Licensed Organisation, then the Assessor may also be the Supervisor. Ideally the Assessor should still meet the appropriate level of independence from the team, particularly at Gold level.		
10	None.	None.	Groups of up to 12 are acceptable where watch teams of up to six are used to ensure that team dynamics remain within the spirit of the Expedition section.
16	It should be noted that towards the end of the season, particularly in higher latitudes, daylight hours are reduced so consideration should be given to ensuring that groups are not benighted.		

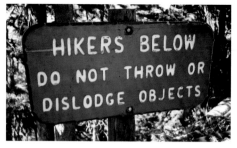

Multiple modes of travel

While the DofE is not against the use of multiple modes of travel, it should be noted that participants must be trained to the required standards in all the modes of travel they use and must still be capable of journeying unaccompanied and being self-sufficient. Minimum adult intervention and the concept of a journey must still be embraced.

Safety

Licensed Organisations are responsible for the safety and well-being of participants. They also approve Supervisors and Assessors and set training, experience and/or qualifications that are required. As a DofE Leader you must ensure that all your LO's requirements are fulfilled. Whilst we do not insist on specific qualifications it is strongly recommended that suitable national qualifications for the chosen modes of travel are obtained.

You, or your chosen expedition provider, are responsible for the suitability of expeditions, safety aspects, the adequacy of the training and emergency procedures. If this is not your LO, then they should ensure that the Approved Activity Provider is reputable, risks have been assessed and that Supervisors and Assessors are suitably competent.

Specific, detailed advice on training, supervision and assessment can be found in the *Expedition Guide* or on EX[2].

We'll now outline additional responsibilities for adults involved in the Expedition section. These are in addition to the overall responsibilities stated in chapter two.

Expedition Supervisors

All expeditions, including practice expeditions, must be supervised by a suitably experienced adult who is competent in the chosen mode of travel and who will be based in the area where the expedition takes place.

Additionally, Supervisors should be familiar with the team, their individual strengths and weaknesses and their knowledge of the chosen route. An understanding of the aims, principles and requirements of the Expedition section is also essential.

Supervisors accept responsibility for the safety and welfare of the team on behalf of the LO. They must be satisfied that participants are capable of undertaking the planned expedition. This is important as the qualifying expedition is unaccompanied. Contact with adults should be kept to a minimum.

As a Leader, if you are not undertaking this role, the Supervisor may help you arrange training for the team using the DofE Expedition Training Framework

Training should only be provided by those who have the necessary skills and experience and are approved by your Licensed Organisation.

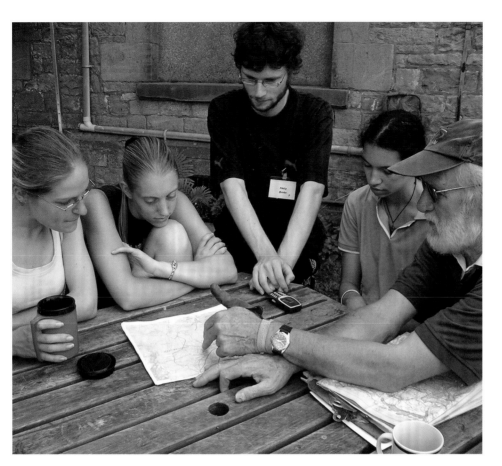

Whilst expeditions are conducted unaccompanied and supervised remotely, Supervisors must always be able to deal with team emergencies.

Supervisors may supervise teams more closely for short periods of an expedition when travelling through potentially hazardous environments.

This must be kept to an absolute minimum and used to allow a team to overcome an unavoidable hazardous area in their expedition route.

At Gold level it should not be necessary for any Supervisor to be present on the same camp site as participants overnight.

If the team does not have the necessary training and skills to operate safely in an area or environment unaccompanied for the duration of the expedition, then they should not be there.

All relevant safety information must be carried by Supervisors. This includes the names, addresses and emergency contact numbers for participants, the Assessor, the home contact, a nominated person in the LO and the DofE's Head Office emergency telephone number (01753 727400).

Expedition Assessors

All qualifying expeditions must be assessed by a competent adult who is approved by your Licensed Organisation and accredited by The Duke of Edinburgh's Award.

The role of the Assessor is to:
- Ensure that the aim of the Expedition section is met.
- Ensure that the 20 conditions of the Expedition section are fulfilled. Assessors are the guardians of the DofE's high standards.
- Assist with the safety of the participants, by advising them on their route, equipment etc. Responsibility for the health and safety and the welfare of participants rests entirely with the Supervisor who is the representative of the Licensed Organisation whilst on the expedition. If there are serious safety concerns, as a last resort, Assessors can withdraw their services, which will bring the assessment of the expedition to an end.

- Protect the interests of the DofE. This is largely achieved by using local knowledge to avoid sensitive areas and friction with certain landowners or overburdened communities.

All Expedition Assessors must be accredited at the appropriate level through The Duke of Edinburgh's Award Expedition Assessor Accreditation Scheme (EAAS). For details, contact your LO or visit **www.DofE.org/training**

In some situations for specialised modes of travel it may be difficult to find an Accredited Assessor with competency and experience in the mode of travel. In these cases it may be appropriate to use an Assessor who works alongside another adult with the specific mode of travel skills, this might be the Supervisor.

Please note:
- At Bronze and Silver level, Assessors should not have been involved in any training or instruction of the team.
- At Gold level, the Assessor must be independent of your DofE group and not associated with the team in any way.

Open expeditions

These enable independent participants, those who missed their own group's expedition or those unable to form a viable team, to complete practice and qualifying expeditions. They include a familiarisation and planning period followed by a supervised and assessed expedition. All necessary training and practice expeditions must be undertaken before a participant can take part in an open qualifying expedition.

Open expeditions in the UK and across the world are offered by Approved Activity Providers, the DofE and LOs. Details are available on our website **www.DofE.org/opportunities**

Approved Activity Providers

We appreciate that not all DofE Leaders want, or are able, to lead expeditions.

 We approve some organisations to deliver training, practice and qualifying expeditions to help groups complete their Expedition section.

Commercial organisations wishing to deliver the Expedition section on behalf of a Licensed Organisation must be an AAP.

See page 115 for further information or visit **www.DofE.org/aap**.

Supporting publications and materials

- Our website (**www.DofE.org/expedition**) contains information including details of the Expedition Training Framework for each level of DofE programme, the notification forms and information about a number of expedition areas.
- Participants, Supervisors and Assessors should use the *Expedition Guide* and EX^2 interactive training as source materials and as a basis for their training programmes.
- Other important information is produced by government departments, national governing bodies and many environmental and conservation organisations.

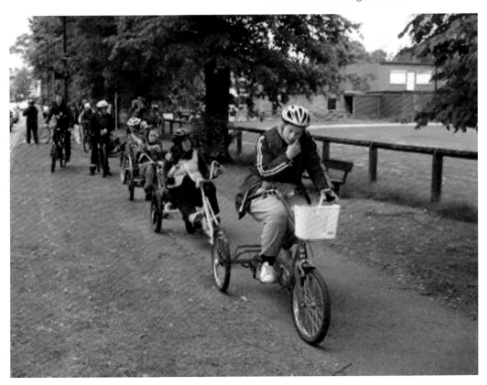

Expedition section ideas

For this section, participants need to identify their expedition aim, mode of travel and location. Listed in each category are examples of expeditions that participants could do.

By foot
Examples:
- Exploring team dynamics and skills with a different team leader each day as they explore the Cairngorms.
- Conducting a study of insects on the South Downs.
- Planning a route in the Lake District to visit areas that inspired three of Wordsworth's poems.
- Considering the impact of tourism on the flora and fauna of the French Alps along your expedition route.
- Following a series of footpaths in the Mourne Mountains, taking photographs to illustrate the Countryside Code to other DofE participants.

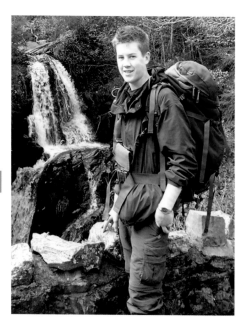

By bicycle
Examples:
- Investigating features and uses of the Thames along the Thames Cycle Path.
- Following part of Gerald of Wales's route of 1188 through Pembrokeshire.
- Measuring heart rate, pulse and calories whilst undertaking a physically demanding expedition in the Cheviot Hills.
- Using the cycle system in the Netherlands to undertake a research project on the provision and quality of cycle paths compared to the UK.
- Exploring 'Constable Country' in Suffolk, visiting places where Constable painted and taking photographs of the current landscape to compare the scenes with the paintings.

By boat
Examples:
- Exploring and photographing the Norfolk Broads using sailing dinghies.
- Planning and completing a cross-channel journey in a yacht and composing a DofE sea shanty.
- On their expedition, using simple mapping techniques to produce their own map of a local estuary and comparing it with a professional map when they return.
- Rowing along the Danube in Germany, looking at the industry along the river.
- Planning and completing a Bronze sailing expedition on Ullswater in the Lake District and producing a video diary of the journey.

By canoe or kayak

Examples:

- Recording the wildlife found on the Strangford Lough canoe trail.
- Taking a series of photos to produce a guide to a section of the Kennet and Avon canal.
- Making a study of the locks and lochs on the Caledonian canal.
- Carrying out a wilderness trip in Canada utilising the canoe trails used by the original settlers.
- Choosing several points along a river and measuring speed of flow, width and depth. Comparing the differences along their route, trying to explain why this may be.

By wheelchair

Examples:

- Following a disused railway track noting the current use of previous railway buildings.
- Producing an illustrated guide to a stretch of canal. Researching the history and then travelling along the tow path using the expedition to gather photographs and sketches to illustrate the guide.

- Planning a route in Cropton Forest and taking a series of landscape photographs to use in a calendar.
- Preparing a user's guide of a country park or National Trust estate, explaining how it can be used, e.g. fishing, picnicking, conservation.
- Planning and undertaking a challenging route in the Peak District, making a short video diary of their experiences.

On horseback

Examples:

- Planning and completing an expedition on horseback across the Marlborough downs investigating Neolithic sites.
- Planning and completing an expedition with sea views in Devon, taking photos along the way so that they can paint a picture of their favourite scene when they return.
- Exploring accessibility and bridle paths in the Brecon Beacons.
- Going on an expedition through wooded areas, noting the different types of trees and age of trees they observe along the way.
- Going on a horse-riding expedition and writing a poem on their return to describe their experiences.

Residential

◼ Residential (Gold level only)

Aim

To inspire participants through a concentrated involvement with people they don't know, who are usually from different backgrounds, and bring alternative views to the challenges they will face. The Residential section broadens their experiences by empowering them to make a difference in a team-based residential setting.

The powerful positive impact on a young person of a well structured residential experience is widely acknowledged. For the DofE this is a fundamental element of Gold DofE programmes, often providing the most important transformational experience for those involved.

Participants could base their experience around an existing interest, for example taking part in a sailing course, developing their photography skills or working on a conservation project. Alternatively they could try something completely new – like working at a kids' summer camp, learning French in Paris or helping to rebuild a school in the Gambia.

Principles

- Residential experiences take young people outside their normal environment and enable them to separate themselves from their daily routine.
- It is a chance to step outside their comfort zone, gain new skills for life, enjoy new experiences and have fun.
- By finding opportunities that interest them away from their usual group of friends, they will develop initiative and planning skills.
- By taking part in a residential, young people will broaden their horizons and develop maturity and independence.
- Interaction with people from different walks of life, ages and backgrounds promotes respect and understanding.
- Completion of shared objectives will develop social and teamworking skills and better prepare them for adulthood.

Benefits

Through completing the Residential section, young people will:
- Meet new and different people.
- Develop the confidence to thrive in an unfamiliar environment.
- Build new relationships and show concern for others.
- Work as part of a team towards shared goals.
- Accept responsibility for themselves and others.
- Develop communication skills and effective coping mechanisms.
- Develop respect and understanding for others.
- Show initiative.
- Develop the skills and attitudes to live and work with others.

What is required?

Participants undertake a shared activity or specific course with people they don't know in a residential setting away from home and in an unfamiliar environment. Evenings are often as much a part of the experience as the daytime activities.

This flowchart gives a simple overview of the steps involved for a young person to complete their Residential section. Each step is explained in more detail on the following pages.

Preparation
Young people identify a residential activity they're interested in doing, where it's taking place and who they'll do it with. They'll set themselves personal goals on eDofE and let the activity provider know they want their participation to count for their DofE programme.

Training
Participants undergo any training/preparation necessary to allow them to take part in the residential.

Activity
Participants join their residential and take part in the activities for a minimum of five days and four nights.

Assessment
At the end of the residential activity, the young person meets with their Assessor to discuss, record and review the quality of their experience. The Assessor provides feedback that can be used in eDofE.

The Handbook for DofE Leaders

In order to give participants every chance of contributing to activities and gaining real benefit, they will usually require briefing or training prior to starting their residential activity.

How long for?

The residential activity should normally take place over at least five consecutive days with a minimum of four nights spent away. In exceptional circumstances, and at the discretion of the LO, this commitment can be spread over two weekends. However, it must involve at least four nights away within a 12 month period, during which the same activity is pursued.

Who they can do it with

This section offers a high degree of flexibility but it must be done with an organised group, registered charity or Approved Activity Provider.

They must join a residential activity individually and not as part of an existing group of friends. It is acceptable to know a few of the others taking part, but the vast majority should not be people

already known to the participant. This should also include the staff running the residential. This is because developing the social skills to establish new friendships and working relationships is an essential part of this section. School or youth group trips are therefore not acceptable.

The group should be no smaller than five people to provide the opportunity to achieve the outcomes of the section. Similarly, all of the group should be on the residential experience as the challenge is to come together with people they don't know to complete the shared activity. Work experience and live-in internships are therefore not acceptable.

Participants generally select a project or activity that will see them stay at an activity centre, with a charity, at a youth hostel or camp, but it could be completely different, for example on a tall ship, boat or barge. Staying with friends or relatives is not acceptable.

There are no age restrictions on the people they can do their residential activity with. For example, conservation projects can attract volunteers of all ages from all over the UK, and your participant may be the only one under 25 or doing their DofE.

As their DofE Leader, you and their chosen activity provider should agree in advance that the opportunity meets the section requirements. If your participant is under 18, you need to ensure that safeguarding principles are paramount.

The activity should provide opportunities for broadening interests and experiences. It is ideal for trying something new, or it can be related to existing interests or activities followed in other sections of a programme. For example, a participant may run an after-school club for children with disabilities for their Volunteering section, and then choose to work on a charity's summer camp for children with disabilities.

Alternatively, for their Skills section, they may develop a promotional DVD for their youth club following a residential videography course.
Practice and qualifying expeditions are not acceptable for the Residential section.

The four steps to completing the Residential section:

1: Preparation is everything

It's vital that the participant thoroughly researches their chosen activity prior to meeting you to discuss their choice. They will then be able to discuss constructively what personal goals should be set.

During the meeting you must also cover:
- What the main purpose of the residential is.
- How it will facilitate their self-improvement.
- Whether the residential meets the requirements and conditions of the DofE.
- Any necessary safety or legal requirements.
- Support or training related to health and safety, skills and awareness.
- The process for evaluation and assessment.
- How the activity and their progress is to be recorded in eDofE and the format of the final review.

Once you are satisfied that the activity and choice of Assessor meets all requirements, you must gain your LO's approval. With this in place, the participant must tell the relevant organisation that they would like their time with them to count towards their DofE programme.

The Assessor should maintain regular contact with the young person and be aware of what they are trying to achieve.

The Assessor should be briefed about the requirements and aims of the Residential section and be given a copy of the guide to the Residential section leaflet.

2: Training to make a difference

Initial training may be required so that young people are safe to take part.

3: Activity, the residential

On arrival at the activity/venue, the participant should remind the course leader that the project will form part of their Gold DofE programme. Meetings should be arranged with the Assessor at the beginning, during and end of the activity to review progress and discuss issues relating to the experience.

4: Assessment, completing the section

The Assessor must remain in regular contact with the participant throughout their residential activity. Once complete, the participant must discuss their experiences with their Assessor who will provide a report which can be used in eDofE.

Participants should be encouraged to add their own comments and other evidence of their experience into eDofE.

Participants should also record:
- How they developed and their progress towards achieving their goals.
- The difficulties they faced and how they overcame them.

Participants will be assessed on:
- Personal standards
- Relationships with others
- Responsibility
- Initiative
- Development of skills
- Knowledge and general progress.

Participants should also have the opportunity to review the quality of experience with their Assessor and enter that report into eDofE, which will then be completed by the Assessor.

If you are not the Assessor then organise a meeting with the participant to review and discuss their experiences when they return.

*Guidance notes are available to download at **www.DofE.org/residential** or from the Resource Zone on eDofE.*

Top five residential considerations to check

The following notes provide information to help you decide the suitability of a young person's choice of residential activity.

Residential considerations	Further explanation
1: The participant must be away from home for a minimum of five days and four nights and must have identified an Assessor.	• Attending a group activity during the day but returning home each evening is not allowed. Participants should stay overnight with the group. Individual home stays or staying with a friend or relative are not allowed. • In most cases this will be consecutive days and nights. In exceptional circumstances, and at the discretion of the Licensed Organisation, the residential could be spread over two weekends in the same 12 month period during which the same activity must be pursued. • Evenings are as important as the day, so participants should be mixing with the group during planned activity and down time. • The Assessor should engage with the participant during the residential and must be familiar with the aims and objectives of the section.
2: There must be a specific, shared course or activity to broaden experiences and interests done with an organised group, registered charity or Approved Activity Provider.	• Doing an activity individually during the day whilst staying in a residential setting with others would not count. • Participants must volunteer their time on the residential and not receive payment; however, they may receive money for expenses. • Work experience and live-in internships are not acceptable. • Going on holiday is not an appropriate activity. The participant should do some form of purposeful activity, such as a training course leading to a qualification, a course which develops skills or interests or which involves volunteering. As with other sections, this should not be an activity which is part of the curriculum. • Participants cannot count their practice or qualifying expeditions for this section.

3: Consider the group size and make up.	• The group should be no smaller than five people (including the participant) who are all on the residential experience, as the interaction with others is crucial to the success of the residential and a group any smaller than this will not provide sufficient opportunities. • Participants should ideally join a residential as an individual. A few participants may know each other when they are joining a larger group, where possible these participants should be separated. • Other members of the group can be of any age. • The staff should also be unknown to the participant (for example, helping Bronze or Silver participants with their expeditions for your school or DofE group is not acceptable).
4: Before the residential, the participant should carry out appropriate training, briefing or research.	• Participants should research the activity that they have chosen and follow any pre-activity instructions or requirements. • In some cases this may mean meeting some of the people on the residential once or twice before the residential for essential training.
5: The Licensed Organisation must have approved the planned residential in advance.	• All residential projects must be approved by the Licensed Organisation in advance of the residential taking place.

Residential section ideas

For this section, participants need to identify an activity that they want to learn, or improve at, from any of the categories below, that is being done away from home.   Participants then need to set themselves objectives and create their programme to meet them.

Service to others

Examples:

- Assisting at a summer camp for Brownies.
- Helping out on a pilgrimage to Sri Lanka.
- Aiding deafblind young people and adults to enjoy a holiday.
- Rebuilding a school roof in Lesotho.
- Being an assistant to support an eco-friendly waste project at an outdoor education centre.

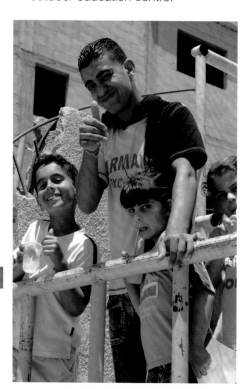

Environment and conservation

Examples:

- Attending a conference on climate change as a youth representative for their local authority.
- Studying coral bleaching in Australia.
- Joining a tree planting project in County Antrim with the Woodland Trust.
- Monitoring the bat population in the New Forest.
- Helping the preservation team of a narrow gauge railway in mid Wales.

Learning

Examples:

- Undertaking a cookery course in France.
- Doing a photography course run by a university and exhibiting their work.

The Handbook for *DofE* Leaders

- Learning to snowboard on an intensive course in Scotland.
- Improving their Spanish language skills on a course in Madrid.
- Learning to write and produce music and putting on a show for local people.
- Taking part in a multi-faith residential, studying different religions and how they interact with each other.

Activity based
Examples:
- Taking part in a week-long discovery of stage combat in Wales.
- Joining an ACF activity week with members of different detachments.
- Joining an historical re-enactment of the Battle of Bosworth.
- Undertaking a week-long course to improve their kayaking skills.
- Travelling to Fiji to become a rescue diver.

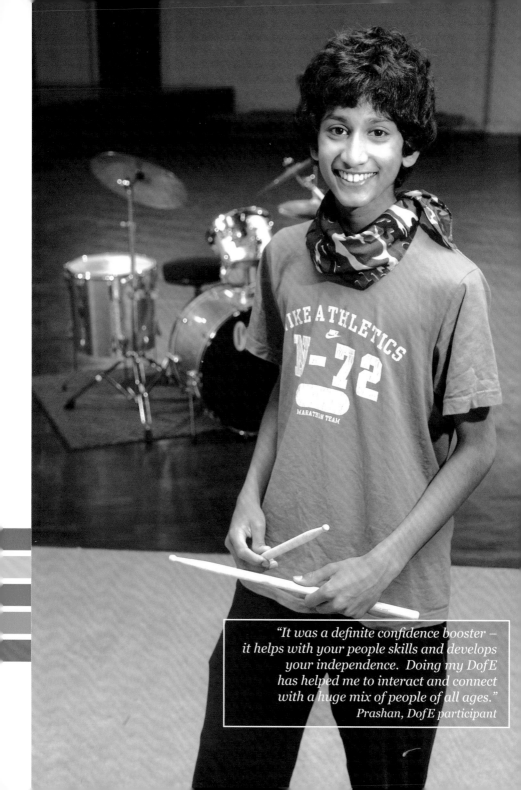

"It was a definite confidence booster –
it helps with your people skills and develops
your independence. Doing my DofE
has helped me to interact and connect
with a huge mix of people of all ages."
Prashan, DofE participant

Chapter 5
Completion, recognition and progression

In this chapter you'll find tips and suggestions to help participants complete their programmes and how to reignite their interest if they're flagging. You can also read about how you can celebrate their achievements and what participants can do after achieving their Gold Award.

Helping participants complete their DofE

When young people start their DofE programme they do so with an expectation that they will complete it and achieve an Award. In fact, it's important to make it clear to them that the expectation is that because they've started, they'll finish.

Whilst we accept that a small number of participants will not see their programme through to the end, it is important that as many as possible do complete it. It is your responsibility as their DofE Leader to help them achieve this. Below you'll find a list of potential reasons why a participant's attendance may waver, along with tips on how to address each situation.

Low motivation

Participants can lose heart or feel less energised about achieving their Award as time progresses. To counteract this or even nip it in the bud, regularly talk with them. Find out how they feel, any problems they may be facing and how they could be solved. Celebrate every achievement when you meet them, through sectional presentations, progress charts, information on noticeboards and high profile Award presentations.

You can monitor progress through eDofE and follow up with participants who are not making the expected progress.

Access to activities

Activities are key to all programmes. A young person's interest may decline if they can't do the activities they want or have problems getting to them. Take time at the beginning to help them choose and record their choices in eDofE.

By taking the time to talk to participants at the beginning you can manage their expectations about what is available. Talk to them about their interests and help them to choose activities that they're genuinely interested in and will be motivated to do.

One way of re-igniting a participant's interest is by organising group activities which encourage a team spirit e.g. fundraising in the Volunteering section. It's also worth trying taster sessions so that they can get a feel for activities they might not normally have considered.

Wrong choice of activity

To avoid this situation arising, make sure you are aware of all the programme guidelines, are up-to-date with all developments within the DofE and of course the manner in which activities are organised. You can do this by visiting our website, reading our magazine for Leaders and e-newsletter, plus any regional newsletters. It's also worth staying in regular contact with your centre's Co-ordinator, your LO and other Leaders in your region. Remember, if you are in doubt about anything, check with your LO.

If a participant feels that they've selected the wrong activity (though it fits the section), don't forget they can change once in each section at each level. Both activities will need to be recorded in *eDofE*.

Only interested in the Expedition section

When you talk with young people about their programme, it's important to impress upon them that ALL the sections offer fun, excitement and adventure.

You may also consider using the Expedition section as encouragement – they can only start it when they finish two other sections; this can often give young people an incentive.

Fear of the Expedition section

At the other end of the scale, some young people may be put off by the thought of an expedition. They may be getting pressure from their peers to do it, be unsure about going to places that are outside their comfort zone or simply feel it's going to be far too tough to do. You can help by talking to them and reassuring them. Remind them that by planning their own route and deciding how they want to travel, they'll be in control and they can ensure that what they're doing is achievable. Talk them through the training they'll be doing and explain how this will prepare them for their expedition. Using EX^2 can be a fun and easy way to do expedition training.

If it's a fear of the unknown, make sure you show them photos of the area and get them to have a look online.

You can also arrange a presentation from some older groups who may have experienced the same fears but still completed their expedition.

Not doing or finishing the qualifying expedition

If participants miss their qualifying expedition or cannot complete it for any reason, you can help them to find an alternative. If you are not planning another expedition there are always places available with other groups. Talk to your DofE Co-ordinator or DofE Manager to find out what is available or check out the opportunities pages on our website.

Lack of kit/equipment

If participants have difficulty getting hold of kit or equipment, check with your centre's Co-ordinator or LO to see if they can help. Sponsorship from local businesses or support from grant awarding bodies may also be a route worth investigating. The DofE provides advice and guidance on expedition kit at **www.DofE.org/go/expeditionkit**

Exams

Given the age of participants it's quite likely that their activities will become disrupted by exams. Obviously you cannot expect their programme to take precedence over these, but during this time you can support them from a distance. Keep in contact via phone, emails, newsletters, social networking sites and blogs, particularly if the exam period has ended. Make yourself available to them so that they know they can achieve their Award after their exams.

Too many other things on the go

From part-time jobs and other clubs, to parties and peer pressure to do other things, many young people find it difficult to fit everything in. With regular mentoring and chats you should be on top of what your participants are doing. Keep a close eye on attendance levels and if things start to drop, chat with them to find out why.

If they are doing too much, it's worthwhile helping them to plan and reprioritise their activities so that they can continue with their programme. They could do one section at a time. It's also worth reminding them that they may already be enjoying activities in their spare time that could count towards their DofE. Try to work with them to see if they can use something they're doing as part of their programme.

Changes in parental circumstances

These can have an emotional and practical impact on a participant's life. If there is upheaval in their family life,

attendance at group meetings may wane and they may find it more difficult to get to and from their activities. By keeping in close regular contact with the young person you'll know about potential problems early on.

You can reassure them and ensure that they are aware that they can always return to their programme at any time if they feel unable to continue for the moment. For some, attendance may prove a good distraction. If they do choose to reduce attendance keep in touch via phone (if appropriate), email and newsletters.

Overprotective parents/ guardians/carers

Of course it's only right that a parent or guardian should worry about the safety and well-being of their child. When you organise a recruitment event take time to talk with them about their concerns. Get parents, carers or guardians of current participants to attend and talk about their experiences too. You can also allay concerns and enthuse them about their child's activities during sectional presentations; so take time to talk to the parents, guardians and carers in attendance.

The Handbook for DofE Leaders

Family holidays, illness and injuries

Always stay in close contact with your participants. Make sure they know that you are ready to help them kick-start activities on their return. If they take time out due to holidays, illness or injury get in touch when they return or recover. Sometimes all it takes is a gentle nudge to get young people back on track.

Lack of transport

If young people are struggling to get to/ from their activities, there are ways you can help:

- Talk to them about changing an activity to one that is more easily reached. Many might not be aware they can do this.
- Help them research local public transport options.
- See if any of your other helpers or older participants could help with transport.
- Other parents within your group may be able to help if young people are doing activities in a similar area – you can facilitate this.

Finances

There are plenty of grant awarding bodies that participants could get in touch with to support them in their adventures, equally local businesses and local authorities can assist too. Make sure participants who are experiencing financial problems are aware of these potential solutions.

Religion/culture

The Duke of Edinburgh's Award is respectful of all cultures and religions. Programmes can be conducted to accommodate all manner of

requirements including all-girl groups and religious festivals. As participants design their own programmes they can be developed to accommodate their unique needs. It's important to point this out when recruiting. Ask parents of participants who might relate to the people you are speaking with to talk about their experiences.

Un-approved activities

Many young people complete all their activities and sections and simply forget to send them for approval on eDofE. Remind them to keep updating eDofE and make sure that you respond promptly with feedback and approvals. As a Leader you can directly approve completed sections on eDofE providing the Programme Planner and minimum timescales have been completed and there is an Assessor's report.

Change/lack of Leader

If you are unable to continue as the DofE Leader for your group, make sure you give your DofE Co-ordinator and/or DofE Manager as much notice as possible, so they can recruit a new Leader. Give them as much help and support as you can to find one and do a handover/training session with the new Leader.

Moving

If a young person is moving out of your area, give them details of their nearest Licensed Organisation. Stay in touch to encourage them to find a new group and complete their programme.

They just need to give their new group Leader their eDofE ID number. The new LO can then transfer their account to the new group.

Sectional certificates

These are available in each section of the Bronze, Silver and Gold levels. They can be issued at your discretion, with the approval of your Licensed Organisation.

These certificates provide participants with tangible recognition of their progress through each section of their

programme. It's also a great way to recognise the achievements of a young person who's unable to complete all sections of their programme. Licensed Organisations can obtain these from **www.DofEshop.org**

Achieving an Award

Completing a programme and achieving their Award gives a participant unique experiences and helps develop the skills and attitudes they need to succeed in life. From start to finish, it's one huge adventure that will stay with them forever.

The great thing is that, as a DofE Leader, you'll play a key role in helping young people achieve an Award. You'll be encouraging, supporting and advising them every step of the way; it's a huge but truly fulfilling responsibility.

To achieve an Award, the participant's eDofE records must be signed off by your Licensed Organisation. In larger LOs, this will be done solely by the DofE Manager or an Assistant DofE Manager, as they are unlikely to have had any direct involvement with the young people completing the programme and so are able to take a completely independent view on the young person's programme.

In smaller LOs (Directly Licensed Centres), a DofE Award Verifier, who has not had direct contact with the young people signs off the completion of the Award. For Gold Awards, these must also be approved by the relevant DofE Regional/ Country Office.

Please see chapter three, page 35, for more details.

Progression

Once one Award has been achieved and celebrated, your key role as a DofE Leader is to encourage participants to progress to the next level.

Respond promptly with feedback and approvals and talk to them about moving up a level. If there is a Participation Place available, the next level can easily be added to the participant's existing eDofE account.

If a young person has only one section left to complete, they meet age requirements and the requirements set out on page 35, you could also get them started on the next DofE level earlier.

Each step up demands more commitment, which is great news for young people who love a challenge. However, it's equally important that you don't leave them feeling overwhelmed at this thought.

Allay any concerns or work out how to overcome any issues or difficulties your participant faced during the level they've just finished, to ensure their DofE experience can be continually improved.

It's also worth reminding your participants that they can choose completely different activities for the next level, or choose to keep getting better at the ones they've just been doing – whatever interests them most!

Certificates, badges and Award presentations

Bronze and Silver Award holders receive a certificate and a badge. Gold Award holders receive a certificate and can choose either a badge or a brooch. Images of these can be found at **www.DofE.org/gold**

Your LO is in charge of deciding how to present Bronze and Silver Awards and many will organise local presentations. If you would also like to arrange one just for your group and/or centre that's absolutely fine, but let your LO know about your arrangements first. Remember, you must wait until the Awards have been authorised and granted by your LO before organising the presentation.

Gold Award holders are invited to a national presentation at one of the Royal Palaces in the presence of either HRH The Duke of Edinburgh or HRH The Earl of Wessex. These are held throughout the year in England, Scotland and Northern Ireland. The date of their Gold Award Presentation may be some time after the participant's Award is confirmed but they'll receive an invitation as soon as possible.

*For details of Gold Award Presentations please see **www.DofE.org/gap***

Lost certificates and badges

Participants can apply to the LO for replacements of any lost Bronze or Silver certificates and badges. There may be a charge for this.

The appropriate DofE Regional/Country Office will deal with any Gold Award badge or certificate replacements, for which there is a small charge. In such cases participants will have to provide evidence that they hold a Gold Award.

Staying involved

For many people, achieving an Award is just the beginning of their DofE journey. The intensely challenging experiences are addictive. Continuing their DofE life as a helper is the way for our Award achievers to stay involved and give something back.

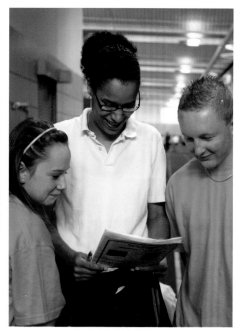

Award holders who've recently achieved their Gold Duke of Edinburgh's Award make excellent DofE Leaders. Some may already have leadership experience, having been DofE Leaders with Bronze & Silver groups for their Volunteering section.

They can also make very inspirational Leaders for participants. This is because participants often relate better to an individual closer to their age who can deal with them on their terms and in their language! Gold Award holders are great role models and give young people something to aspire to.

To help your participants develop onto the next stage in their DofE experience, why not introduce them to the DofE Leadership Programme? It will help shape their leadership skills and strengthen their knowledge, equipping them to be a fantastic DofE Leader.

See **www.DofE.org/training** for more details on the DofE Leadership Programme and other modules that the DofE offers.

> *"The most important attribute I got from doing the DofE was gaining confidence and learning about my strengths. I have been a volunteer Leader for about five years, which has really developed my confidence and I will continue to develop the DofE wherever I am. I feel the DofE has given me so much and I would like to give something back!"*
> *Louise, Gold Award holder*

So, once you've got their attention, what can you do?

- Run an 'open evening' and leadership taster sessions.
- Give them meaningful, specific roles for example to support specific participants through eDofE.

"The young people at my DofE centre are always talking about the importance of recycling. When a group of them achieved their Gold Awards recently, I suggested they 'recycle themselves'. They are now really enjoying helping the next generation of participants through their programmes."
Ian Jones, DofE Leader

- Use them as ambassadors to go out to speak to potential participants.
- Provide them with training opportunities. Training courses may be provided by you, your centre or your LO.
- Point them to training opportunities such as the DofE Leadership Programme: **www.DofE.org/training**
- If they're moving away, help them get in contact with their local LO in their new area. Encourage them to keep in touch.

It is important that new Leaders understand their role and responsibilities, particularly if they have recently been a participant in the same group. All Leaders are expected to follow the DofE's Code of Behaviour *(see page 118)* and ensure that their relationships with participants are appropriate.

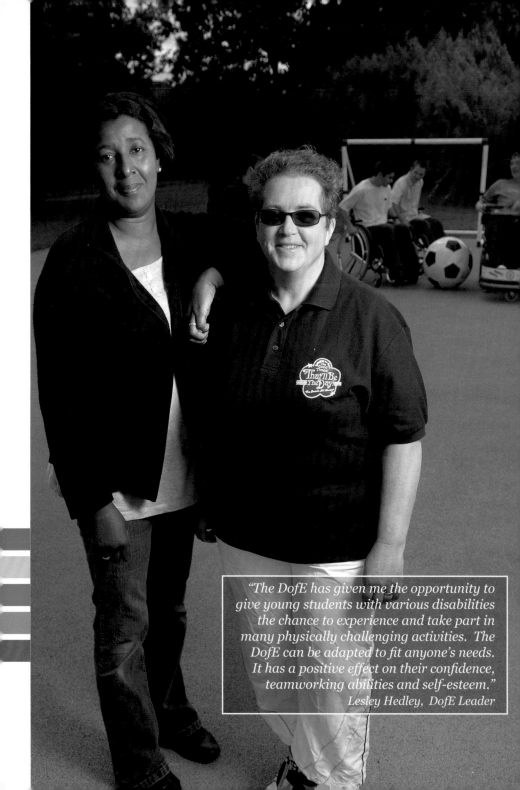

"The DofE has given me the opportunity to give young students with various disabilities the chance to experience and take part in many physically challenging activities. The DofE can be adapted to fit anyone's needs. It has a positive effect on their confidence, teamworking abilities and self-esteem."
Lesley Hedley, DofE Leader

Chapter 6
Other important information and sources of support

This chapter provides you with information about support, training, our partners, our international network and guidance on DofE policies.

Empowering young people

We never forget that young people are at the heart of everything we do.

The DofE encourages Licensed Organisations, Co-ordinators and Leaders to involve participants individually, within their peer groups or through forums, in considering how best to use DofE programmes to address:
- The issues that affect their lives.
- How the DofE programme is delivered to help meet those needs.
- How resources are allocated to support that process.

"It's important for programmes such as the DofE to help young people develop. It's very important for Asian young people to take part in the DofE as the social skills gained mean that it's easier to fit into society. It allows people of all backgrounds and races to take part in things that they would otherwise not have the opportunity to do."
Sumiya, Gold Award holder

Support from your Licensed Organisation

Your Licensed Organisation is always your main source of support. They will authorise your appointment and support you during the set up of your group.

LOs will clarify the range of services and support they provide through their induction training. This includes the responsibilities outlined in their Licensed Organisation Licence but, in general, you can expect the following:

Ongoing support

Your LO will keep you informed about developments within your area and any programme opportunities. They can let you know how to get hold of any specialist equipment that your participants might need and assist you in organising Award presentations.

As you can imagine, leading a DofE group and/or centre requires administration, so in addition to eDofE, which supports the administration of participants' programmes, your LO can provide you with help to keep things running smoothly. They will also provide you with training, promotional and support material, along with *Welcome Packs*.

Many Licensed Organisations offer imaginative ways of support to help participants complete their Awards, for example:
- A weekly surgery for anyone who needs advice and guidance.
- Support from a Development Worker when you have a new group.
- Extra advice and information sheets (see the Resource Zone on eDofE for national and local resources).
- Certificates of thanks for centres that have high completion rates.

Check with your LO to see what they will do to help you.

Training for success

The success of DofE programmes relies on the effectiveness of people like you – DofE Leaders who run them. It's your competence and confidence that provides inspirational, high quality experiences for the thousands of young people who aim for an Award.

Your training is an integral part of this support as it enhances the experiences of all participants. This is why we believe everyone should receive quality training according to their needs at local, regional and national levels. In turn this will:

- Achieve consistency in the delivery of programmes to young people.
- Promote and share good practice.
- Support organisations and individuals in the delivery and development of the DofE programmes.
- Keep individuals up to date with new methods of delivery, changes to any criteria and to the DofE Charity itself.

Your LO is responsible for providing suitable learning opportunities for you and your volunteers. This will include an induction as well as regular, appropriate training, support and recognition whilst involved with the DofE.

You may also have access to a range of non-DofE-specific training opportunities through your Licensed Organisation including, for example, safeguarding and child protection, technical skills training and diversity.

Some of this training can lead to qualifications in youth work and outdoor activities. It may involve meetings, courses, conferences, online and distance learning provided by your LO or DofE Regional/Country Office. Accreditation for Expedition Assessors is also available through the DofE's Expedition Assessor Accreditation Scheme (EAAS).

You'll find details of the training opportunities available from LOs and DofE Regional/Country Offices at **www.DofE.org/training**

Remember, your Licensed Organisation is there to help you. So if you do have any questions or need assistance, just get in touch.

You can also choose to receive our monthly e-newsletter, which delivers the most up to date and relevant information straight to your inbox.

Sign up for both on eDofE through your profile preferences, or at **www.DofE.org/leaders**.

eDofE

eDofE provides access to the latest news, communication and resources as well as useful information to help you manage your group. Support on using eDofE can be obtained within eDofE.

Support from the D*of*E Charity

Website

We provide a wide range of useful resources to help run your DofE group and to promote your activities. For information on everything including current training opportunities, fundraising and the latest expedition advice, visit **www.DofE.org** and keep an eye on the news and resources pages in eDofE.

You'll also find plenty of free downloadable guidance notes on the site at **www.DofE.org/sections** *For answers to some of the most common questions we get asked, please visit* **www.DofE.org/faq**

Communications

Don't forget to sign up for a free subscription copy of our magazine for DofE Leaders, which is published three times per year at the start of each academic term.

The DofE Modular Training Framework

We created the DofE's Modular Training Framework to give Leaders access to a wide range of flexible, relevant and high quality training opportunities. This guides our trainers and aides our voluntary helpers to understand what is available and what skills they can expect to gain.

The framework also means that any training you do is transferable if you move groups – so be sure to ask your LO if they use it.

You can find details of the Modular Training Framework at **www.DofE.org/training**

Current modules include:
- e-induction
- Introduction to the DofE
- The DofE Leadership Programme:
  - Managing a DofE group
  - Teamwork & Leadership skills
  - Practical DofE Leadership
- Expedition Supervisor
- Expedition Assessor Accreditation
- Train the trainer.

e-induction

We have developed an online e-induction programme for any potential or existing DofE Leader. This is free to use and can be accessed at **www.DofEtraining.org** – it's the ideal training resource for any new helpers and a good refresher for anyone who's been a DofE Leader.

It will help them understand essential information about the DofE and may be used by some LOs as a pre-requisite for other courses they are running.

Getting your activities noticed

Naturally, you'll need the right resources to promote your group and activities. So for posters and leaflets – available at nominal cost – email our trading arm, ASL, at **asl@DofE.org** or have a look at what's available at **www.DofEshop.org** Your LO or centre may also provide material to help you.

All Licensed Organisations, approved centres and groups can use the DofE logo – available at **www.DofE.org/logo** along with guidelines on how it should be used. On that page you can order free bespoke logos for your group.

DofE groups and centres are instrumental in generating local publicity and attracting new entrants and helpers.

Publicity for the DofE can be achieved by:

- Celebrating young people's achievements in your local communities at presentation events and through the local media.
- Publicising information on when your group meets.
- Promoting the activities and successes of your group/centre.
- Engaging the active support of local sponsors and key community figures.

You can find sample press releases etc. at **www.DofE.org/press**

Expedition Areas and Co-ordinators

Taking part in our wild country expeditions can provide your participants and you with some of the most exhilarating and exciting DofE experiences and memories. But, this will only happen if it's well planned and prepared.

Our expedition networks provide local advice and guidance to help with your preparation.

For a list of Expedition Areas and Co-ordinators visit **www.DofE.org/expeditionareas**

Please see chapter four for details on procedures for communicating with Expedition Areas and Co-ordinators.

Complaints, feedback and enquiries

We define a complaint as when a person wishes to formally register their dissatisfaction with the information or service provided by The Duke of Edinburgh's Award, or the manner in which they were treated.

Most complaints, feedback or enquiries can be dealt with locally by you, the DofE Leader, your DofE Co-ordinator or a DofE Manager at your Licensed Organisation.

Where this is not possible a procedure is set out on our complaints, feedback and enquiries system, which can be accessed at **www.DofE.org/feedback**

If you receive a complaint, please deal with it promptly.

Members of the public are unlikely to be able to distinguish between the levels of responsibility within the DofE. If you cannot deal with it, please contact your Licensed Organisation, who, if necessary, will refer it to their DofE Regional/Country Office.

If it is a child protection issue, The Duke of Edinburgh's Award and Licensed Organisation Child Protection policy and procedures take precedence, and should be implemented immediately.

The International Award Association

This is the governing body for all countries that offer DofE programmes, including the United Kingdom.

DofE programmes now operate in over 120 countries under a variety of titles including, for example, The International Award for Young People, The President's Award, and The National Youth Achievement Award. Whilst the title may vary, the underlying philosophy and basic principles of operation are the same.

Further information can be obtained from The International Award Association: **sect@intaward.org**

www.intaward.org

Links with other programmes

Participants can use experiences gained with other organisations as part of their programme. This can include, for example, voluntary and community organisations, secondary, independent and special schools, colleges and universities, young offender institutions, pupil referral units, housing associations, open DofE groups and businesses. Activities followed through these partner organisations may count towards their DofE programme, as long as they satisfy the relevant conditions and requirements.

Approved Activity Providers

The Duke of Edinburgh's Award licenses external organisations that provide opportunities for the Expedition and Residential sections. These opportunities have been proven to meet our conditions and so can count towards the achievement of an Award. We call these partners Approved Activity Providers (AAPs).

They can be commercial organisations or charities and are usually able to provide a section in its entirety, including accredited assessment and providing reports on eDofE. As a DofE Leader, you can confidently recommend AAPs to your participants. Commercial organisations wishing to deliver the Expedition section on behalf of a Licensed Organisation must be an AAP.

The AAP licence is a quality standard on an organisation's activity, meeting the programme and sectional requirements of the DofE.

Please note that the AAP licence does not guarantee the suitability of an AAP in terms of health and safety or its financial stability. Licensed Organisations using AAPs will have their own process for checking the suitability of AAP programmes in terms of health and safety requirements for their young people and they have the final say on the appropriateness of a course in this respect.

*You'll find a list of current Approved Activity Providers at **www.DofE.org/aap** together with details of how organisations can apply for this status.*

Commercial partners

If a company produces, distributes or retails high quality products that participants could use to help achieve their Award, they can become a DofE licensed commercial partner. In return, we:

- Provide them with a DofE partner logo, which can be used to promote their association with us.
- Allow them to promote their products to LOs, DofE centres/ groups and participants.

Endorsed products must meet our quality standards and be suitable for our participants and helpers.

For more information on our current commercial partnerships, please visit **www.DofE.org/lifezone**

"Working with participants with special needs is really rewarding. It's great that they are able to participate with their able-bodied friends as equals. I didn't know whether I'd be able to cope but when you see what these young people do and temper that with their ability, or lack of, it's rewarding to see how they progress."
Barry Sinclair, DofE Leader

DofE policies

You must ensure that you and your group abide by the following DofE policies.

Equal opportunities

Never forget that DofE programmes are about inclusion not exclusion. They can be designed to meet the needs of any young person, whatever their ability.

There is no room for discrimination within the DofE. And by that we mean treating a person less or more favourably than another on the grounds of age, race, colour, ethnic origin, nationality, gender, marital status, sexual orientation, disability, health, creed, religious beliefs, class, financial status or caring responsibilities.

Furthermore, we do not discriminate on the grounds of criminal convictions or political beliefs that do not conflict with the aims, principles and policies of the DofE.

Your LO will have its own Equal Opportunities Policy that you must follow too.

If you ever have to ask a participant to leave the group you must inform them that they will remain registered with The Duke of Edinburgh's Award until their 25th birthday. You may be able to help them find a new way to complete their programme. If you need any assistance, your LO or DofE Regional/ Country Office will be able to help.

Safeguarding and child protection

it is the policy of The Duke of Edinburgh's Award to safeguard the welfare of all young people and others involved in DofE activities by protecting them from physical, sexual and emotional harm.

The Duke of Edinburgh's Award accepts and promotes that in all matters concerning child protection, the welfare and protection of the young person is the paramount consideration.

Safeguarding is about planning and organising activities to prevent potential harm or damage to young people. Child protection is concerned with protecting and/or removing a young person from physical, sexual, emotional abuse or neglect.

The DofE and your Licensed Organisation have Safeguarding and Child Protection policies and procedures in place. You must ensure that you and any other adults working with you on the DofE are aware of and abide by these.

In particular you must know and understand the steps they should take if they become aware of, suspect or receive allegations of abuse, harassment or bullying.

"I was more than happy to deal with the bit of paperwork to be CRB checked, because it gives parents more peace of mind that their child is in a safer environment."
Sarah Hadley, DofE Leader

Code of Behaviour for DofE Leaders and helpers

All Leaders and helpers involved with The Duke of Edinburgh's Award should follow the Code of Behaviour below. You should make sure that everyone in your team is familiar with it. They must also understand your LO's Safeguarding policy and procedures, in particular the steps they should take if they become aware of, suspect or receive allegations of abuse, harassment or bullying.

All Leaders and helpers involved with The Duke of Edinburgh's Award must:
- Treat everyone with respect
- Act as a good role model of appropriate behaviour.

You must:
- Ensure at least one other person is present when working with a participant or at least be within sight or hearing of others.
- Provide separate sleeping accommodation for DofE Leaders and participants during expeditions and residential activities.

- Remember that actions, remarks and gestures can be misinterpreted, no matter how well intentioned.
- Provide access for participants to talk through any concerns they may have.
- Encourage participants to feel comfortable and care enough to point out attitudes or behaviour they do not like.
- Recognise that caution is required, particularly in sensitive moments.
- Not permit abusive youth peer activities (e.g. initiation ceremonies, ridiculing, bullying, harassment etc.).
- Not have any inappropriate physical or verbal contact with others.
- Not jump to conclusions about others.
- Not react to inappropriate attention seeking behaviour such as tantrums or crushes.
- Not exaggerate or trivialise harassment or child abuse issues.
- Not show any favouritism.

You can download copies of our Code of Behaviour at **www.DofE.org/leaders**

Bullying and harassment

It is the DofE's policy that whilst involved in the programme all young people, Leaders and helpers are entitled to an environment free from bullying and harassment. You will have support from your LO and the DofE in addressing any type of harassment or related inappropriate behaviour you or they encounter.

Bullying and harassment, in general terms, is unwanted conduct affecting the dignity of an individual or group of individuals. It may be related to age, sex, race, disability, religion, nationality or any personal characteristic of the individual and may be persistent or an isolated incident. The key is that the actions or comments are viewed as demeaning and unacceptable to the recipient. Your Licensed Organisation is there to help you to deal with any allegations of bullying. If an incident occurs you should seek their support in ensuring that it is dealt with appropriately.

How you can help participants if bullying is occurring

DofE programmes encourage young people to develop their self-confidence and become constructive members of society. Bullying and harassment are unacceptable and taken very seriously. Please feel free to share the following advice on bullying and harassment to your participants and group at large:

- If you feel you are being bullied, whether it is in person, by email, text or online, talk to someone you trust.
- Serious bullying, for example, threats of a physical or sexual nature, should be reported to the police.
- If you can, make a note of the time and date of any incidents.
- Don't forward abusive texts, emails or images to anyone. You could be breaking the law just by forwarding them. If they are about you, keep them as evidence. If they are about someone else, delete them and don't reply to the sender.
- Don't reply to bullying or threatening messages or emails – this could make matters worse. It also lets the bullying people know that they have found a 'live' phone number or email address. They may get bored quite quickly if you ignore them.
- Don't give out your personal details online. If you're in a chatroom, try not to give away any personal information, such as where you live, the school you go to, your email address, etc.
- Don't give out passwords to your mobile phone or email.
- Never bully anyone, or send any bullying or threatening messages. Anything you do, write or send could be reported to an adult.

Remember that sending abusive or threatening messages is against the law.

Care for the environment

The Duke of Edinburgh's Award aims to provide a programme of development for all young people long into the future. Therefore, sustainability of our environment is essential. In light of this we have developed an environmental impact policy, which we all commit to.

The environmental impact policy aims to:
- Promote sustainable use of the outdoor environment.
- Enhance partnerships with the wider community.
- Educate participants about the natural environment and local area.
- Conserve global resources.

Promoting sustainable use of the outdoor environment

- Exercise care and concern for the environment, in line with the Countryside Code.
- Monitor locations used for environmental damage.
- Consider modifying the use of locations to reduce damage.
- Consider assisting with the repair or maintenance of sites, especially if our activities have significantly contributed to that damage.

Enhancing partnerships with the wider community

- Respect the interests of others, especially those who live, work, manage or carry out their recreation in the environment of our activities.
- Comply with bylaws and access agreements.
- Liaise with landowners, local communities and other organisations over any activities, which may affect them or the land over which they have control, or an interest in.
- Be sensitive to the potential and actual impact of our operation on an area or community.
- Follow the Countryside Code.

Educating participants about the natural environment and local area

- Promote awareness and respect for the natural environment.
- Encourage greater understanding of the natural world and the cultural setting of their surroundings.
- Educate participants as to the appropriate way to enjoy, explore, move or live in the countryside.

Conserving global resources

- Reducing our use of global resources and recycling waste products.
- Using products and materials that support the ethos of the DofE.
- Using materials from sustainable sources and recycled materials.
- Using environmentally efficient methods such as eDofE and other online resources.

"I really enjoyed doing my DofE –
it's been an experience I won't forget.
I most enjoyed playing football and
learning woodworking skills."
Josh, DofE participant

Appendices
Other useful information

DofE contact details

Contact details for Licensed Organisations can be found at: *www.DofE.org/takepart*

www.DofE.org

Regional/Country DofE Offices
(Addresses and telephone numbers can be found on www.DofE.org/contact)

- **Scotland:** scotland@DofE.org (**www.DofE.org/scotland**)
- **Northern Ireland:** nireland@DofE.org (**www.DofE.org/nireland**)
- **Wales:** wales@DofE.org (**www.DofE.org/wales**)
- **Central England:** centralengland@DofE.org (**www.DofE.org/centralengland**)
- **South East:** southeast@DofE.org (**www.DofE.org/southeast**)
- **South West:** southwest@DofE.org (**www.DofE.org/southwest**)
- **North East:** northeast@DofE.org (**www.DofE.org/northeast**)
- **Yorkshire & Humber:** yorksandhumber@DofE.org (**www.DofE.org/yorksandhumber**)
- **North West:** northwest@DofE.org (**www.DofE.org/northwest**)
- **London:** london@DofE.org (**www.DofE.org/london**)
- **The Duke of Edinburgh's Award – Head Office:** info@DofE.org (**www.DofE.org**)
- **National Fundraising Team:** supportus@DofE.org (**www.DofE.org/supportus**)
- **The Award Scheme Ltd (ASL):** asl@DofE.org (**www.DofEshop.org**)
- **The International Award Association:** sect@intaward.org (**www.intaward.org**)

Glossary of roles and D*of*E terminology

Achievement Pack

A book containing pictorial evidence and records of a young person's activities undertaken as part of their DofE programme, compiled through *e*DofE.

Assessor

An adult who checks on a young person's progress and agrees the completion of a section of their programme. They will provide an Assessor's report to confirm this (see below).

In the Expedition section, qualifying expeditions must be assessed by a competent adult who is approved by the Licensed Organisation and accredited by The Duke of Edinburgh's Award Charity. Some Assessors are members of volunteer networks which are managed directly by the DofE. Each network is based in a wild country area and members provide a service for Licensed Organisations, assessing expedition teams. For more details see **www.DofE.org/go/expeditionareas**

Assessor's report

An Assessor's report is completed by the Assessor for a particular section of a participant's programme. It constitutes a review of the activities that the young person has been carrying out and documents their progress towards their goals. The report can be recorded online via the DofE website (**www.DofE.org/assessor**), a voice recording, or using the *Keeping Track* booklet.

Award holder

A young person who has achieved a Duke of Edinburgh's Award by completing their DofE programme.

Directly Licensed Centre (DLC)

A Directly Licensed Centre is a type of Licensed Organisation which holds a licence to deliver DofE programmes to young people on its own premises. Directly Licensed Centres can include schools, youth clubs and young offender institutions, which do not run their DofE provision under a licence provided by an Operating Authority.

DofE Business

A DofE Business is a type of Licensed Organisation which offers a DofE programme to a number of its employees.

DofE Award Verifier

In Licensed Organisations, a DofE Award Verifier is appointed to grant final approval to Awards. They are completely independent from the delivery of the DofE programme to the young people.

DofE centre

A location where the DofE is run, for example, a school, youth centre or young offender institution. There may be one or more groups at a centre.

DofE Co-ordinator

The person who sets up and manages the DofE in a centre. They support the Leaders and oversee the groups.

DofE group

A group of young people who are working together on their DofE programmes, with one or more DofE Leaders.

DofE Leader

The adult responsible for a DofE group. They lead, guide and encourage young people, agree their programme choices and sign off *Keeping Track* booklets and their *eDofE* evidence.

DofE Manager

The named person in a Licensed Organisation who is responsible for the day-to-day delivery of the DofE. There will often be other assistants, administrators and staff involved.

DofE team

This is to describe participants who are working on a specific sectional activity. For example: a Silver expedition team will have four to seven participants or a Bronze volunteering team may have three working on a recycling project.

eDofE

The online system for managing young people's progress through their DofE programmes.

Expedition Supervisor

A Supervisor is essential for the Expedition section as they are responsible for supervising and supporting a team of participants to ensure their safety and well-being whilst they are doing their expedition.

Expedition Training Framework

The Expedition Training Framework consists of a number of areas in which young people must prove their competency before they can undertake their DofE expedition. This skills training helps to ensure their safety.

Helper

Any adult who volunteers to help a DofE Leader run a group. They may give general support, i.e. administration, help run one section or give specific training.

Licensed Organisation (LO)

Licensed Organisation is the umbrella term used for the four different types of organisation that can hold licences to deliver DofE programmes. The four different types of organisation are:
- Directly Licensed Centre (DLC)
- National Operating Authority (NOA)
- Operating Authority (OA)
- DofE Business Partner

Modular Training Framework

The DofE maintains a number of training modules to help all adults involved in the DofE to develop the skills that they need to carry out their role effectively. Collectively, these modules are referred to as the Modular Training Framework.

National Operating Authority (NOA)

A National Operating Authority is a type of Licensed Organisation which holds a licence to deliver DofE programmes to the young people with whom they work in one or more of the UK nations.

Operating Authority (OA)

An Operating Authority is a type of Licensed Organisation which holds

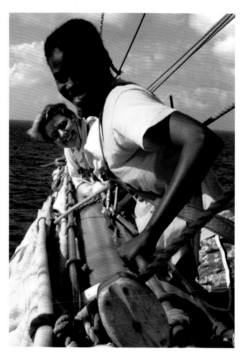

the licence to deliver DofE programmes in a specified geographic area. Operating Authority licences are often held by local authorities.

Participant

Any young person doing a DofE programme.

Participation Place

To take part in the DofE, participants pay a nominal participation fee for which they are allocated a Participation Place within eDofE. The current charge for participation can be found at **www.DofE.org/go/costs**

Welcome Pack

Once a participant has paid their participation fee, they will receive a DofE *Welcome Pack* which contains information and advice on the DofE, their programmes and eDofE.

Index

A

B

C

D

E

F

G